WHOM DO MEN SAY THAT I AM?

Insights Into the Unique Nature of Jesus Christ

Harold Ballew

Whom Do Men Say That I Am?
Copyright 2019© Harold Ballew
All rights reserved. Printed in the U.S. A. No part of this publication may be reproduced, stored in a retrieval system, or transmitted in any form, by any means, without the prior written consent of the copyright owner.

Scripture quotations, unless otherwise noted, are from the King James Version (KJV). The author added bold, italics, and emphasis. It is in the public domain.

Amplified Bible(R), Copyright (c) 1954, 1958, 1962, 1964, 1965, 1987 by The Lockman Foundation, La Habra, CA 90631, All rights reserved.

The Holy Bible, New International Version® NIV®, Copyright © 1973 1978 1984 2011 by Biblica, Inc. ™ All rights reserved worldwide.

Scripture quotations marked WEY are from the *Weymouth New Testament* by Richard Francis Weymouth, 1912, in the Public domain in the United States.

Scripture quotations marked YLT are from *Young's Literal Translation* and are in the public domain.

Scripture quotations marked Strong's Concordance are in the Public Domain.

Scripture quotations marked Bible in Basic English (BBE) are in the Public Domain.

References from Strong's Concordance are in the Public Domain.

References from Vine's Dictionary of New Testament Words, 1940, are in the public domain.

Dedication

This book is dedicated to the members of the Brotherhood Christian Church. Together, in our youthful enthusiasm, we sought to worship and serve the Lord. And we did.
Christine and I are proud to have been a part of this community of believers.

Table of Contents

Chapter 1	**The Early Beliefs**	8
Chapter 2	**The Councils**	16
	First Council of Nicaea	20
	First Council of Constantinople	22
	First Council of Ephesus	23
	Council of Chalcedon	24
	Second Council of Constantinople	25
	Third Council of Constantinople	25
	Second Council of Nicaea	25
	Divisions Remained	28
Chapter 3	**The Creeds**	31
	The Apostle's Creed	31
	The Nicene Creed	32
	The Athanasian Creed	33
	Person in the Creeds	34

	The word person in the Greek NT.	39
	The word Coeternal in the Creeds	43
Chapter 4	**The Trinity**	51
Chapter 5	**The History of the Trinity**	54
	Tertullian	54
	Origen	55
	Novatian	56
	Arius	56
	Athanasius	57
Chapter 6	**Is Jesus Christ God or a "god?"**	59
	Sharp's Rule	65
Chapter 7	**God Is One**	68
	Echad	70
	Yachid	74
	Yāchad	75
	The Number One	77
	Monos	79
	The Godhead is in Jesus Christ	83

Chapter 8	**Father, Son, and Holy Spirit**	89
	The Father	88
	The Son	91
	The Son of God	92
	The Only Begotten	94
	The Son of man	96
	The Holy Spirit	96
Chapter 9	**Problems Examined**	108
	Who raised Jesus from the dead?	109
	Who placed the ministries?	110
	Who indwells the believer today?	111
	Who answers prayer?	111
	On whom shall we believe?	112
	The prayers of Jesus Christ	112
	The Right Hand of God	116
Chapter 10	**A Contradiction Resolved**	124
Chapter 11	**God's Glory Hidden in a Tent**	134

	The Form of God	146
Chapter 12	**Two Witnesses Speak**	149
Chapter 13	**The Mystery of the Name**	155
	The Compound Names	159
	One Name	161
	Elohim	163
	Elohim in the New Testament	165
Chapter 14	**The Lord He is God**	171
Chapter 15	**The 1 John 5:7-8 Controversy**	180
Chapter 16	**Conclusion**	184
Appendix A	Heresy	191
Appendix B	Additional notes on the Trinity	193
Appendix C	The Beliefs	195
Appendix D	Jehovah's Witnesses	196

Introduction

  Jesus Christ is the only person in recorded history who is both God and man. There is no one to compare Him to. How can we understand this unique person? The "key" to understanding Jesus is His dual nature. He is both God and man. While that may sound simple, it is not. Following the apostolic age, Jesus' dual nature ignited a centuries-long debate regarding His deity. Is Jesus Christ God manifest in the flesh? Or is He a "god?" Was He merely a miracle worker? Prophet? Teacher? The church Fathers, after several centuries, settled on what is commonly known as the doctrine of the Trinity. Were they correct?

  In my quest to answer that question, I used several resources, e.g., the Bible, Hebrew and Greek lexicons, the writings of the early Church Fathers, historical documents, and contemporary sources. My work encompasses a brief, influential history of the church councils. It also includes numerous creeds, short biographies of some of the church Fathers, and word studies in the original languages. My conclusions are based on the overwhelming evidence I discovered through my research. I hope to share the evidence in a meaningful and understandable way.

Harold Ballew

Chapter 1
Early Beliefs

"When Jesus came into the coasts of Caesarea Philippi, he asked his disciples, saying, Whom do men say that I the Son of man am?" Matthew 16:13

The apostle Matthew records an odd question Jesus asked of His disciples. The question is found in Matthew 16:13 *"When Jesus came into the coasts of Caesarea Philippi, he asked his disciples, saying, Whom do men say that I the Son of man am?"* Some, they answered, thought He was John the Baptist, others Elias or Jeremiah, or one of the other prophets. Their answers revealed the confusion that existed among the people in Jesus' day. Who was He?

When people are asked, "Who is Jesus Christ?" the answers are also mixed. While some people think Jesus is a myth, most people believe Jesus was a real person. But that's where the consensus ends. Among those who believe He existed, there is a significant difference of opinion about "who" He is. Some believe He was a miracle worker; others see Him as a great moral teacher or prophet of God. Some believe Jesus is merely a "god." Who is He?

Historical Views on the Nature of Jesus (33-100 A.D.)

During the early years of the Christian church, several distinct beliefs about Jesus emerged. The five most prominent were:

1. Monarchianism (Modalism/Oneness):

This is considered the earliest view. Monarchianism teaches that the Father, Son and Holy Spirit are not separate persons but rather different "modes," "titles," or "manifestations of the one God. It denied that the Son and Holy Spirit were separate persons. This teaching is both the earliest and the most enduring one.

2. Arianism:

Arius (ca. 256-336 AD) taught that Jesus was divine but distinct from God the Father, having been created ex nihilo ("out of nothing"). This belief led to the concept of subordination, i.e., the Son is subordinate to the Father.

3. Semi-Arians:

Emerging around 300 AD, Semi-Arians believed that the Son was "of a similar substance" (homoiousios) to the Father, but not of the "same substance" (homoousios). And remained subordinate to the Father.

4. Binitarianism:

Sometimes associated with Semi-Arianism, Binitarianism proposed a "two-ness" of God, focusing on the Father and the Son, but notably did not include the Holy Spirit as a distinct person (ca. 325 AD).

5. Trinitarianism:

Trinitarians believe in three "coequal" and "coeternal persons" within the Godhead: Father, Son and Holy Spirit.

Initially, early formulations did not include the Holy Spirit; this aspect was developed and formalized later, particularly beginning with the Council of Nicaea in 325 AD.

It is important to note that these beliefs were proposed over 200 years after the public ministry of Jesus Christ and the Apostles. Out of this confusion, two beliefs survived. They are Monarchian and Trinitarian. Of the two, the doctrine of the Trinity is well-known, widespread, and embraced by most Christians. However, Monarchianism, more commonly known as Oneness, is less well-known and less widespread. In my experience, the word "Oneness," as opposed to Trinitarianism, among evangelical Christians, tends to be misunderstood. Some evangelicals consider it heretical (see Appendix A). However, the Scriptures and history tell us that the Oneness belief is not heretical. With that thought in mind, I offer a brief historical overview of the Oneness belief.

Oneness: "the fact or state of being unified or whole, though comprised of two or more parts." Briefly stated, it is believed that the Father, Son, and Holy Spirit are three manifestations of the One God. This belief is opposed to the Trinitarian doctrine of three distinct, coeternal, coequal persons in the Godhead.

Oneness belief is not "new" or "novel." It has historical roots that predate the doctrine of the Trinity. Among the first post-apostolic "Oneness" believers were the Monarchians or Modalists. Though there were three notable adherents to Modalism: Noetus, Praxeas, and Sabellius, Modalism would become known as Sabellianism. The problem with ascribing Modalism to Sabellius is this: his opponents destroyed his writing. Virtually everything we know about Sabellius comes from his opponents.

According to the Encyclopedia Britannica, there were two types of Monarchianism: 1. Modalistic, also known as Modalism, and 2. Dynamic, also known as Adoptionism.

Modalistic Monarchianism taught that God was one while appearing (working) through the different modes of Father, Son, and Holy Spirit. They believed all the Godhead dwelled in the person of Jesus. They also believed the Holy Spirit was not a person but God in action. The Modalist/Monarchian belief predated the Trinitarian view by over one hundred years. We know that Modalists were in the majority during Tertullian's time. Tertullian, a church father, ca. 155-240, wrote: " ... gave evidence that the majority of Christians were Monarchian when he noted their startled reaction to his teaching of three in one" (Against Praxeas, chapter 3).

That Modalistic Monarchianism was the dominant belief among Christians in the early church is found in the following quote: "The International Standard Bible Encyclopedia also declared that God's Apostolic Church was in the majority in the 3rd and 4th centuries. It stated, "Monarchianism identified the Father, Son, and Spirit so completely that they were thought of only as different aspects or different moments in the life of the one Divine Person, called now Father, now Son, now Spirit, as His several activities came successively into view, almost succeeded in establishing itself in the 3rd century as the doctrine of the church at large...." (1)

This quote supports my belief that what we now call "Oneness" (Modalistic Monarchianism) was the dominant belief in the first two hundred years of the church! Modalists pointed to the scriptures and concluded that the only number ascribed to God in them was one.

The second type of Modalism, known as Adoptionism, taught that God was one, but it also taught that Jesus was a man "adopted" into godhood. Notable adherents were Theodotus of Byzantium and Paul of Samosata, Bishop of Antioch. This belief fell out of favor.

In the early 20th century, Modalism (not Sabellianism) reemerged. The year was 1913; the place, just outside of Los Angeles, California; the event, the Arroyo Seco Worldwide Camp meeting of Pentecostal preachers. During an otherwise typical service, one preacher, R.E. McAlister, "casually mentioned" that the Apostles always baptized in the Name of the Lord Jesus Christ. Further, he stated that the triune formula of "Father, Son, and Holy Ghost" was never used in baptism. The "new" issue was destined to become a hotly debated one. Early the next morning, one of the preachers in the camp meeting ran throughout the camp, awakening everyone, proclaiming he had been "given a glimpse of the power of the Name of Jesus." (2). The next day, they spent searching the Scriptures.

The following year, many of America's foremost preachers were re-baptized in the Name of Jesus. However, baptism in Jesus' name did not capture the hearts of most people. This new move of God developed a small crack that grew into a split. The "New Issue" or "Oneness movement" was the chief reason, as men grappled with scripture versus traditional theology. Here is one account of what happened: "About the time of World War I, when Pentecostal organizations like the Assemblies of God were organized, a doctrinal controversy that had originated on the west coast swept through the heartland of the United States, especially around St. Louis and Indianapolis. The "New Issue," "Oneness," or "Jesus only," as the doctrine is called, contended that true baptism must be in the name of Jesus only, rather than in using the traditional Trinitarian formula. Furthermore, the proponents of this view denied that there were three persons in the Godhead, asserting instead that there were three manifestations of one person, Jesus". (3)

For a time, this teaching threatened to topple the newly formed Assemblies of God because many of its leaders - men like H.G. Rodgers, Eudrous N. Bell, Howard A. Goss, and Daniel C.O. Opperman - submitted themselves for rebaptism in "Jesus' Name." The denomination withstood the "Unitarian" onslaught within its ranks and, at its fourth General Council in St. Louis (1916), prepared a "Statement of Fundamental Truths." The right to draft such a statement (staunchly trinitarian) was challenged by the "oneness" contingent on the grounds that the formative council at Hot Springs had declared that the Scriptures alone were to be the "all-sufficient rule for faith and practice," and here, a man-made creed (the Trinity) was proposed. The rest is history; the Assemblies of God followed traditional thought, rejecting this new move of God. The "oneness" believers formed their organizations.

Footnotes Chapter 1

1. The International Standard Bible Encyclopedia Vol. V. Page 3022

2. V. Syanan, The Holiness-Pentecostal Movement in the United States, page 154 (Eerdmans).

3. J. Nichol, The Pentecostals, page 116 (Logos)

Chapter 2
The Councils

"Let the man who would hear God speak, read Holy Scripture."
Martin Luther

No central authorities, formal doctrines, or rituals existed during apostolic times. I would add that there was no Pope. Despite the Catholic claim that the Apostle Simon Peter was the first Pope, he was not. While it is true that the Apostles met in Jerusalem to decide whether Gentiles should keep the Mosaic laws (Acts 15), the council was held there, not in Rome. Appointing local elders and leaders is evident in Paul's letter to Titus: *"For this cause left I thee in Crete, that thou shouldest set in order the things that are wanting, and **ordain elders in every city**, as I had appointed thee:"* (Titus 1:5). Each locale, city, or town had its church (people, not buildings) and local leaders, e.g., Timothy in Ephesus, Titus in Crete, and Philemon in the Colossian church. While the early church had apostles, Elders, and local leaders, they recognized Jesus as the head of the church, not an ecclesiastical appointee or Pope.

Paul evidences this by addressing his letters to individual churches. Paul did not write to, or on behalf of, a united church. Most of Paul's letters were written to a specific church. The same is true of the Apostle John. In Revelation, Jesus instructs John to write to the seven churches of Asia: *"Saying, I am Alpha and Omega, the first and the last: and, What thou seest, write in a book, and send it unto the seven churches which are in Asia; unto Ephesus, and unto Smyrna, and unto Pergamos, and unto Thyatira, and unto Sardis, and unto Philadelphia, and unto Laodicea."* (Revelation 1:11). Interestingly, Jesus did not write one letter to all seven churches. He had John write seven different letters. Each one is unique to that specific church. In the letters, Jesus addresses their failings and strengths.

As I wrote earlier, aside from the meeting in Jerusalem (Acts 15), there is no central church hierarchy in the New Testament. There is no record of a central church council ever meeting again during the time of the apostles. History records no church councils met until the Council of Nicaea in 325 A.D. History records seven "major" church councils; I believe there were eight. The first one occurred around 48 AD. It is recorded in the book of the Acts of the Apostles, commonly referred to as Acts. Some refer to this council as the Apostolic Council. We read about it in Acts chapter 15.

This council of apostles and elders convened in Jerusalem to resolve a dispute regarding Gentile converts. While Paul was ministering in Antioch, some "brethren" from Judea told Paul the new converts (Gentiles) needed to be circumcised and keep the laws of Moses to be saved. Paul and Barnabas disagreed, so they agreed to go to Jerusalem to settle the matter: *"When therefore Paul and Barnabas had no small dissension and disputation with them, they determined that Paul and Barnabas, and certain other of them, should go up to Jerusalem unto the apostles and elders about this question."* (Acts 15:2). When they arrived in Jerusalem, they told the church about the conversion of the Gentiles. Again, the Pharisees, who had become believers, argued that the Gentiles needed to be circumcised and to keep the law of Moses. After much discussion, James renders their decision: *"Wherefore my sentence is, that we trouble not them, which from among the Gentiles are turned to God: But that we write unto them, that they abstain from pollutions of idols, and from fornication, and from things strangled, and from blood."* (Acts 15:19-20). Interestingly, this council did not raise the question of Jesus' deity. Following the council of Elders in Jerusalem, there would not be another council for 277 years.

After almost 300 years, another council was convened. This one, however, was convened by the emperor, the political leader Constantine the Great (272-337AD), not by church leaders. He presided over the council of Nicaea (325 AD). More importantly, whatever doctrines the church leaders agreed upon had to be approved by Constantine. He alone held the power to decide what would become orthodoxy in the church. Constantine the Great was a Roman Emperor who ruled from 306 to 337 A.D. He was the first Roman Emperor to become a Christian. However, he waited until his deathbed to be baptized, believing that baptism would absolve him of all his sins committed during his lifetime. He is noted for legalizing Christianity in 313 A.D., thereby ending the persecution of Christians (the Edict of Milan). Galerius (emperor of the Tetrarchy) previously protected Christian's right to practice their religion, but it did not restore their property. The Edict of Milan, issued under Constantine, restored property to Christians. Still, it did not make Christianity the official state religion. It is noteworthy that the edict was not limited to the Christian church; it also granted freedom of worship to cults and other religions.

In 321 A.D., Constantine legalized Sunday as the "venerable Sunday," a day of rest for all citizens of the Empire. In 325 A.D., Constantine convened the first Council of Nicaea. The council set a precedent for succeeding church councils, as succeeding Emperors would also have complete authority over the councils and their decisions. In 337 A.D., he fell ill. When he realized how sick he was, he determined to go home to Constantinople. He did not make it. He died in Nicomedia. Curiously, Constantine requested that Eusebius, a Christian supporter of Arianism of Nicomedia, be his baptizer. Today, Constantine is venerated as a saint by both the Roman Catholic and the Eastern Orthodox churches. They also remember him as the one who had the Church of the Holy Sepulchre built in Jerusalem on the reputed site of Jesus' tomb.

In their rush to confer sainthood upon him, they seem to have forgotten that Constantine had his son Crispus poisoned and his wife, Fausta, murdered. Both murders occurred in 326 A.D., one year after convening the Council of Nicaea. Remember, this man convened and controlled the Council of Nicaea!

The following provides a chronological list of the councils and their contributions to the development of Trinitarian doctrine.

First Council of Nicaea, 325 A.D.

At the Council of Nicaea, they debated many issues, including the date of Easter and the recognition of the See (Bishop) of Alexandria's authority to extend it to other churches. However, due to an emerging school of thought espoused by Arius, the council's chief focus was the nature of Jesus Christ. Arius taught that Jesus was a "creature" distinct (separate) from the Father. Arius taught that Jesus was "begotten" by God the Father at a point in time; therefore, he was "subordinate" to the Father. In response to the Arian teaching, the council produced the Nicene Creed. In doing so, the council introduced the early idea that would become known as the doctrine of the Trinity.

The council decided the Father and the Son are "homoousios," of the "same substance or essence." The council excommunicated Arius and his followers. Here is part of the ruling made by the emperor after the council: "In addition, if any writing composed by Arius should be found, it should be handed over to the flames, so that not only will the wickedness of his teaching be obliterated, but nothing will be left even to remind anyone of him. And I hereby make a public order that if someone should be discovered to have hidden a writing composed by Arius and not to have immediately brought it forward and destroyed it by fire, his penalty shall be death. As soon as he is discovered in this offense, he shall be submitted for capital punishment ...." (Edict by Emperor Constantine against the Arians). Despite the Emperor's edict against Arius and his teachings, when Constantine lay on his deathbed, he requested that Eusebius of Nicomedia baptize him. Eusebius was an Arian! Apparently, the Emperor did not have any deep conviction regarding the Godhead.

The question for historians was this: "Did Constantine convene the council for 'purity' of doctrine or to maintain the 'unity' of his empire? Some historians believe that Constantine feared the Arius controversy would split the church and undermine the empire's unity. The following quote may reveal Constantine's motives: "Council of Nicaea, also called First Council of Nicaea (325), the first ecumenical council of the Christian church, meeting in ancient Nicaea (now İznik, Turkey). It was called by the emperor Constantine I an unbaptized catechumen. He presided over the opening session and participated in the discussions. He hoped a general council of the church would solve the problem created in the Eastern church by Arianism, a heresy first proposed by Arius of Alexandria that affirmed that Christ is not divine but a created being. Pope Sylvester I did not attend the council but was represented by legates." [1] I believe that Constantine had political motives for convening the council. He wanted to maintain unity between his kingdom's eastern and western parts.

Though the Bishops had agreed that the Father and Son shared the same "substance, essence," they did not include the Holy Spirit. The inclusion of the Holy Spirit was addressed later at the First Council of Constantinople (381), when the Holy Spirit was recognized as "of the same substance, essence" with the Father and the Son. If the "trinity" is found in the scriptures, why did they fail to include the Holy Spirit, the "third person of the Trinity"?

An interesting note regarding Constantine, upon his death, two of his sons split the empire. Constantine II (Western provinces) remained pro-Nicene. His brother, Constantius (Eastern provinces), was an Arian, thus anti-Nicene. The third brother, Constans, would become ruler of the Western provinces upon the death of his brother Constantine II. Constans continued to support the Nicene orthodoxy. The question of "who is Jesus" was not resolved at the Council of Nicaea. In the following fifty-five years, the dispute remained. This dispute led to the next council.

First Council of Constantinople, 381 A.D.

This council was convened by Emperor Theodosius (Eastern Empire), a committed believer in the Nicene Creed. All attendees were from the Eastern Church; none were from the Western Church. It approved the Nicene Creed, corrected an "oversight" of the Council of Nicaea by acknowledging the divinity of the Holy Spirit, and made Christianity the empire's official religion. In the Edict of Thessalonica, the Trinity, as understood at the time, was established as the official doctrine of the state and the church. Here is a quote from that council: "It is our desire that all the various nations which are subject to our Clemency and Moderation, should continue to profess that religion which was delivered to the Romans by the divine Apostle Peter, as it has been preserved by faithful tradition, and which is now professed by the Pontiff Damasus and by Peter, Bishop of Alexandria, a man of apostolic holiness. According to the apostolic teaching and the doctrine of the Gospel, let us believe in the one deity of the Father, the Son, and the Holy Spirit, in equal majesty and in a holy Trinity. We authorize the followers of this law to assume the title of Catholic Christians; but as for the others, since, in our judgment, they are foolish madmen, we decree that they shall be branded with the ignominious name of heretics and shall not presume to give to their conventicles the name of churches. They will suffer in the first place the chastisement of the divine condemnation and in the second the punishment of our authority which in accordance with the will of Heaven we shall decide to inflict." (2) They may have believed the issue was settled, but it was not!

First Council of Ephesus, 431 A.D.

Emperor Theodosius II (401-450 A.D.) convened the council. The council dealt with the teaching known as Nestorianism. Nestorius, Archbishop of Constantinople from 428 to 431 A.D., raised two issues. First, he believed and taught that the Word and Jesus were not the same. The Word was God, eternal, whereas Jesus was of the flesh, not eternal. He taught that they "came together in a hypostatic union," a union of divine and human natures in a single person.

Nestorius also challenged a long-held belief regarding Mary, the mother of Jesus. At the time, Theotokos, "bearer/mother of God," was a popular term in the Western Church (including Constantinople). It was used to refer to Mary, but not in Antioch. Nestorius maintained that Mary should be called Christotokos, "bearer/mother of Christ," not Theotokos, "bearer/mother of God." The council rejected Nestorius' claim and proclaimed Mary as the "Theotokos" or "Mother of God."

Council of Chalcedon 451 A.D.

Emperor Marcian (392-457 A.D) convened the council of Chalcedon. It was the fourth ecumenical council of the Christian Church, held in Chalcedon. The Council affirmed that Christ is "the same perfect in Godhead and also perfect in manhood; truly God and truly man." He is "consubstantial [homoousios] with the Father according to the Godhead, and consubstantial with us according to the Manhood." Jesus Christ is "to be acknowledged in two natures, in confusedly, unchangeably, indivisibly, inseparably." The divine and human natures of Christ are distinct yet united in one person. This co-existence of Christ's two natures is known as the hypostatic union. The council also affirmed that Jesus Christ is fully divine and fully human. He is the Son of God (1John5:10) and the Son of Man (Mark 14:21). (www.gotquestions.org/council-of-Chalcedon.html).

Finally, it ratified the creeds of Nicaea and Constantinople. In doing so, it condemned the false doctrines of Nestorius and Eutyches. The Council of Chalcedon anathematized (cursed) those who taught Christ had only a single, divine nature.

Second Council of Constantinople, 553 A.D.

The Byzantine Emperor Justinian convened the council. Of the 152 attendees, only 16 were bishops from the Western church. The remaining bishops were from the Eastern church. The purpose of this Council was to reiterate the Church's support for the Chalcedonian Creed and the condemnation of Nestorianism. They also condemned the teachings of Origen, i.e., the pre-existence of souls, etc. During this council, the emperor imprisoned Pope Vigilius, further demonstrating the emperor's control over the councils. For this reason, some refused to accept the council's decrees due to political pressure from the emperor.

Third Council of Constantinople, 680 A.D.

At this Council, convened by Constantine IV, the church addressed the doctrine known as Monothelitism. i.e., Jesus had two natures but only one will. The church believed Jesus had two wills, one human and one divine. These, they thought, corresponded to Jesus' two natures.

The Second Council of Nicaea, 787 A.D.

This council was the last by the Eastern Orthodox and Roman Catholic Church. The Empress Regent Irene of Athens convened it. It was initially held in Constantinople. It moved to Nicaea after soldiers attempted to disrupt the council. The topic: the veneration of "icons" or so-called "holy images." Earlier, the Emperor, Constantine V, banned the practice (iconoclasm). The church wanted to restore its use of them. It was determined that "As the sacred and life-giving cross is everywhere set up as a symbol, so also should the images of Jesus Christ, the Virgin Mary, the holy angels, as well as those of the saints and other pious and holy men be embodied in the manufacture of sacred vessels, tapestries, vestments, etc., and exhibited on the walls of churches, in the homes, and in all conspicuous places, by the roadside and everywhere, to be revered by all who might see them. The more they are contemplated, the more they move to the fervent memory of their prototypes. Therefore, it is proper to accord to them a fervent and reverent adoration, not, however, the veritable worship which, according to our faith, belongs to the Divine Being alone–for the honor accorded to the image passes over to its prototype, and whoever venerates the image venerates in it the reality of what is there represented." (3) The council also decreed that every church should contain a relic. A relic consists of a saint's remains or the saint's personal effects. Relics are kept for veneration as a physical "memorial."

It is important to note that these councils, convened by emperors, not church leaders, ultimately formulated the doctrine of the Trinity. Second, the emperor convened and controlled every council, not the church leaders. Third, these councils also established: the date of Easter (Passover), that Priests should not marry, that Christianity was the State religion, that Mary was the mother of God, and that venerating dead Saints and relics was not only permissible but encouraged.

Summary of the Councils:

Nicaea 1	defined the divinity of Jesus. Formulated the beginnings of the Trinity.
Constantinople I	defined the divinity of the Holy Spirit. Emperor Theodosius made Christianity the official religion of the empire.
Ephesus	Defined Jesus as the Incarnate Word of God. Mary was proclaimed Theotokos or Mother of God.
Chalcedon	defined Jesus as God and Man in one person.
Constantinople II	reconfirmed the doctrine of the Trinity. They condemned Nestorianism.
Constantinople III	Reconfirmed Jesus' humanity with two natures, i.e., human and divine.
Nicaea II	approved the veneration of icons, "holy images," and relics.

A final thought. Though the church leaders met in councils, their decisions were not binding without the emperor's approval. The emperor influenced their final decisions and creeds.

Divisions Remained

To make matters worse, the churches were still divided. The Assyrian Church (East) only recognized the first two councils. However, the Oriental Orthodoxy church recognized three. The Catholic and Eastern Orthodox churches rejected the Fourth Council of Constantinople. Deep divisions persisted despite numerous attempts to produce a united church and doctrine. For example, there remains a deep divide between the Western and Eastern churches. It concerns the Latin word "Filioque." The word means "and the Son" in Latin. The word does not appear in the original text of the Niceno-Constantinopolitan Creed. In the original Creed, the Holy Spirit proceeded from the Father. It did not have the words "and the Son" in the creed.

The Western church adopted this rendering, "and the Son," while the Eastern church used "through the Son." Thus, the words "the Holy Spirit proceeded" were added to "from the Father through the Son." The Eastern church prefers this construction over the Western church's "from the Father and the Son." Here is how it is written in the creed: "I believe in the Holy Ghost, the Lord, the giver of life, who proceedeth from the Father (and the Son). Who with the Father and the Son is adored and glorified." This illustrates the difficulties the early church faced in defining the nature of God. The disagreement that caused the split between the

Western and Eastern churches remains. With that in mind, let us look at what the church finally settled on as its Creed.

Footnotes Chapter 2

1. www.britannica.com/event/council-of-nicea-christianity-325

2. Codex Theodosianus XVI.1.2

3. www.newworldencyclopedia.org/entry/Second Council of Nicaea

Chapter 3
The Creeds

"No creed can be stretched to the size of truth .... "
Lemuel K. Washburn

We know that the early Church Councils devoted a great deal of time and energy to resolving the question(s) regarding the deity and humanity of Jesus Christ. Throughout many hundreds of years, the church developed several "creeds." These creeds would become the "touchstone" of orthodoxy in the church. If one were to be accepted as a believer by the church, they would have to embrace its creeds. By some accounts, the church created eight creeds over the years. The oldest is known as the Apostle's Creed.

The sheer number of councils and creeds suggests to us, again, that the debate over the nature of Jesus Christ was never universally agreed upon by the church fathers. The following are the established creeds. I chose not to publish all of them as that would be extensive. Instead, I have opted to publish the popular ones. As you read the following creeds, you will see that the doctrine of the Trinity was never biblical; it evolved over many years.

The Apostle's Creed (180 A.D.)

The Apostle's Creed does not explicitly address the divinity of either Jesus or the Holy Spirit. It was believed to have been written around 180 A.D. Still, no authorship is attributed: "I believe in God, the Father almighty, creator of heaven and earth. I believe in Jesus Christ, God's only Son, our Lord, who was conceived by the Holy Spirit, born of the Virgin Mary, suffered under Pontius Pilate, was crucified, died, and was buried; he descended to the dead. On the third day he rose again; he ascended into heaven, he is seated at the right hand of the Father, and he will come to judge the living and the dead. I believe in the Holy Spirit, the holy Catholic Church, the communion of saints, the forgiveness of sins, the resurrection of the body, and the life everlasting. Amen." (1)   Though this creed is known as the Apostles' Creed, it was not written by any Apostle.

The Nicene Creed (325 A.D.)

The Council of Nicaea adopted the Nicene Creed, describing Christ as "God of God, Light of Light, very God of very God, begotten, not made, being of one substance with the Father." The creed used the term homoousios (of one substance) to define the relationship between the Father and the Son. After over fifty years of debate, "homoousios," of one substance, was recognized as the hallmark of orthodoxy and was further developed into the formula of "three persons, one being." I mentioned previously that the Confession of the Council of Nicaea failed to include the divinity of the Holy Spirit. Athanasius developed the doctrine of the divinity and personality of the Holy Spirit in the last years of his life: "We believe in one God, the Father Almighty, Maker of all things visible and invisible. And in one Lord Jesus Christ, the Son of God, begotten of the Father the only-begotten; that is, of the essence of the Father, God of God, Light of Light, very God of very God, begotten, not made, being of one substance (ὁμοούσιον) with the Father; by whom all things were made both in heaven and on earth; who for us men, and for our salvation, came down and was incarnate and was made man; he suffered, and the third day he rose again, ascended into heaven; from thence he shall come to judge the quick and the dead. And in the Holy Ghost. But those who say: "There was a time when he was not;" and "He was not before he was made;" and "He was made out of nothing," or "He is of another substance" or "essence," or "The Son of God is created," or "changeable," or "alterable"—they are condemned by the holy catholic and apostolic Church." (2)

The Athanasian Creed

The Athanasian Creed was developed in either the late fifth or early sixth century. Though it is called The Athanasian Creed, it was not written by him. At the time of the council, Athanasius had been dead for many years. Some historians believe the creed was named after him because of his early influence on the doctrine of the Trinity. "Whosoever will be saved, before all things, it is necessary that he hold the catholic Faith. And the Catholic faith is this: that we worship one God in Trinity, and Trinity in Unity; neither confounding the Persons, nor dividing the essence. For there is one Person of the Father; another of the Son; and another of the Holy Ghost. But the Godhead of the Father, of the Son, and of the Holy Ghost, is all one; the Glory equal, the Majesty coeternal...." "And in this Trinity, none is before, or after another; none is greater, or less than another. But the whole three Persons are coeternal and coequal. So that in all things, as aforesaid: the Unity in Trinity, and the Trinity in Unity, is to be worshipped. He therefore that will be saved, let him thus think of the Trinity ...." (3). Here we read the words "Trinity," "person," and "coeternal" used in the creed.

The Athanasian Creed differs from earlier creeds by including anathemas and condemnations of those who reject it. Interestingly, the Creed was accepted in Western churches but rejected by the Eastern churches. While the doctrine of the Trinity was firmly planted in the "soil" of the church, questions remained; if the doctrine of the Trinity is "in the scriptures," why did it take so long to "find" it? Why did the church leaders convene the many councils? Why the protracted debates?

Persons in the Creed (s)

The introduction of the word "person" into the creeds presents an interesting study. The word person had an entirely different meaning in the fourth century than it does today. The word person, as used in the Athanasian Creed, comes from the Greek word "prosopon" or the Latin word "persona." These words meant "a mask or a face." One common use of the Greek word "prosopon" described the mask that an actor used in a Greek drama. One actor might use several masks (prosopon) as the drama unfolded. But the word "prosopon" referred to the mask and its character, not to the actor or person. Unlike masks, we can see God's real character in the person of Jesus Christ.

In this sense, the early writers may have envisioned one God with one will and one purpose, manifesting Himself through the "masks" of the Father, Son, and Holy Spirit. The only distinct and separate parts were the "masks" (or, as the Bible says, manifestations 1 Timothy 3:16), not God. Using "persons" as "masks" is much more acceptable than how modern theologians and Christians have interpreted the word "person" today.

Today, we find a different meaning for the word "person." Funk and Wagnalls Standard Desk Dictionary lists the following as the first definition for the word person: "1. Any human being considered as a distinct entity or personality; an individual." The word "entity" means "independent, separate, or self-contained existence." Today, men use the modern definition of the word "person" and apply it to the Godhead, not the original word, i.e., "prosopon" (masks). In doing so, they have perhaps unwittingly introduced tritheism.

The Nicene Creed did not use the word persons, as the following quote shows: "the familiar Nicene Creed which is recited in certain Christian churches today, it should be said, is not the original creed adopted at Nicaea in 325 A.D., but an expanded form of it (often called the Constantinopolitan Creed) which came into use after the time of the General Council of 381. John B Noss wrote: "For completeness, we may add that the later formulation says firmly that the Godhead of Father, Son, and Holy Spirit is 'one in essence' (or substance), though in three hypostases (subsistence or individualized manifestations). When this formulation was translated into Latin, the rather abstract Greek word for individualized manifestations became the rather concrete word "persona," and connotations of distinct and self-contained personality were suggested in a way not intended by the original Greek wording." (4) Note the following in the quote: "… when this formulation was translated into Latin, the rather abstract Greek word for individualized manifestations became the rather concrete word persona, and **connotations of distinct and self-contained personality were suggested in a way not intended by the original Greek wording.**" This may be the "smoking gun," as to how the belief of "persons" became part of the creed.

As I wrote earlier, the Athanasian Creed introduced the word "person" into the Trinitarian doctrine. Today, the Athanasian Creed is not used in most churches. The significance of this creed is that it is the first to explicitly state the equality of the three persons of the Trinity. It is believed to have been written in the late fifth or early sixth century. This would put it at least 100 years after Athanasius. Here is another portion of the creed: "… So, there is one Father, not three Fathers; one Son, not three Sons; one Holy Ghost, not three Holy Ghosts. And in this Trinity, none is before or after another; none is greater or less than another. But the whole three Persons are coeternal and coequal. So that in all things, as aforesaid; the Unity in

Trinity, and the Trinity in Unity, is to be worshipped. He, therefore, that will be saved, let him thus think of the Trinity."

In this creed, the idea of separateness is introduced using the words persons, Trinity, coequal, and coeternal. While the Athanasian Creed was generally accepted, it was not universally accepted. Some churches did not adopt the trinitarian belief; instead, they held to the original belief in one God without separation. The Athanasian Creed typifies the church's ongoing struggle to clarify the Godhead. Still, it has brought confusion that persists to this day. It declares the separateness of God and, in the next breath, declares His oneness.

Even the reformer Martin Luther, the founder of the Protestant movement, had a problem with the word "person" in the Trinitarian creed. We read: "on the word persona, (etc.) Much has been said, about the time of the Reformation, concerning the tendency of these terms to lead to tritheism. Among the advocates for their expulsion from theological disquisition might be mentioned a number of the first divines of the age, not excepting Minnius and even Luther himself. To prevent the charge of Arianism or Socinianism, which he knew his enemies would eagerly seize the least pretext to prefer against them, Luther yielded to Melanchthon's wishes, and in the Augsburg Confession, the doctrine of the Trinity is couched in the old scholastic terms." (5)

Luther, a Trinitarian, advocated removing specific terms because they might lead to tritheism, i.e., the belief in three gods. Though he recognized the inherent error in using the word "persons," he chose to accept it rather than contest it. Sadly.

A final word on the use of "persons" in the Trinity. Karl Barth, who is considered by many to be the "greatest Protestant theologian of the twentieth century" and the most prolific, rejected the use of the word "persons." Barth preferred "modes of being (seinweise)." Barth believed the use of the word "persons" was outdated, as it suggests "three personalities in God." He writes, "This would be the worst and most extreme expression of tritheism, against which we must be on guard at this stage." He remained a Trinitarian, though some accused him of being a modalist, a charge he denied. (6) Mr. Barth is not alone.

The desire for doctrinal conformity and imperial unity led to the church councils and the creation of creeds. The fact that men met, debated, and produced a Creed does not necessarily mean they were correct. It only means the majority agreed after a much-spirited debate and, I would add, dissent. After the Creed (s) were decided upon, those who disagreed were labeled heretics. In a bizarre twist of history, among those labeled as heretics were some who made significant contributions to the creation of the Trinity. Tertullian, who was the first to use Trinitas (Trinity/Eng.), would later be labeled a heretic. Origen, who contributed the idea of the "eternal generation" of the Son to the doctrine of the Trinity, would be excommunicated. Novatian, who determined the Holy Spirit was the third person in the Godhead, was also excommunicated.

The Word person in the Greek New Testament

The doctrine of the Trinity uses the word "person" in describing the Father, Son, and Holy Spirit. How does the Bible use the word "person?" Strong's (4383) Greek "prosopon" occurs 78 times in the New Testament. It is translated as face 55x, person 7x, presence 7x, countenance 3x, and not translated 1x.

In Hebrews 1:1-3, Jesus is described as the "express image of His person." This suggests that God was described as a "person" in the scriptures: *"God, who at sundry times and in divers manners spake in time past unto the fathers by the prophets, Hath in these last days spoken unto us by his Son, whom he hath appointed heir of all things, by whom also he made the worlds; Who being the brightness of his glory, and the express image of his **person**, and upholding all things by the word of his power, when he had by himself purged our sins, sat down on the right hand of the Majesty on high;...."*

Does the word "person," here referring to God, tell us God is a "person"? The word translated as "person" in this passage is not the one generally used for "person." The Greek word for "person" is "prosopon." In this passage, a different Greek word was translated as "person." It is "hypostasis" (Strong's 5287). This word, hypostasis, could have been rendered "substance" or "essence." God, apart from the incarnation, is Spirit (John 4:24), not one of three persons in the Godhead. This passage properly refers to God's "substance" or "essence," not a "person."

Jesus is described as "the express image of His person." The words "express image" are a translation of the Greek word "character." It appears only here in the Bible. It means "the figure stamped, i.e., an exact copy or [figurative] representation." (Strong's Talking Hebrew and Greek Dictionary) The American Standard Version translates "the express image of His person" as "the very image of his substance." The Bible in Basic English has "the true image of his substance." Jesus is the "very image of his (God's) substance."

Two passages in the King James Version of the Bible refer to Jesus Christ as a "person" (prosopon). The first one occurs in Matthew 27:24. Here, Pilate calls Jesus a "just person." The word "person" is not in the Greek text. In the Greek text, the word translated as "person" is "dikaios," meaning: "righteous, just, right, or meet." Young's Literal Translation translates it as *"... I am innocent from the blood of this **righteous** one."* Here is the second passage. It is the only time the word person (prosopon) is applied to Christ: *"To whom ye forgive any thing, I forgive also: for if I forgave any thing, to whom I forgave it, for your sakes forgave I it in the person of Christ;"* (2 Corinthians 2:10) It is possible, though not probable, that the writer meant "person" when he used the Greek word prosopon in this passage. It is more probable that he meant "sight" or "presence" rather than a person. However, if the writer meant to use the word "person," it would be acceptable as Jesus Christ was a person, the only person in the Godhead.

However, using the word "person" to describe God would not be correct, as God was never a "person" or "man." Jesus taught that God is Spirit, not a person. Therefore, most translations use the words "face" or "presence" when God is the subject, e.g., Acts 3:19, *"Repent ye therefore, and be converted, that your sins may be blotted out when the times of refreshing shall come from the **presence (prosopon)** of the Lord;"* Young's Literal Translation reads: *"reform ye, therefore, and turn back, for your sins being blotted out, that times of refreshing may come from **the presence of the Lord**,"*

We see the same translation in Revelation 6:16: *"And said to the mountains and rocks, Fall on us, and hide us from the **face (prosopon)** of him that sitteth on the throne, and from the wrath of the Lamb:"* Young's Literal Translation reads: *"and they say to the mountains and to the rocks, `Fall upon us, and hide us from **the face of Him** who is sitting upon the throne, and from the anger of the Lamb,"* Again, in the book of Hebrews 9:24, we read: *"For Christ is not entered into the holy places made with hands, which are the figures of the true; but into heaven itself, now to appear in the presence of God for us:"* In this passage, it would be incomprehensible to translate it as "… now to appear in the person of God for us". The translators have it right, i.e., "presence."

In the Old Testament, we have the word "paniym," which may be translated as "person." The translators realized that the Greek word prosopon was translated correctly as "face" or "presence" (sight, countenance, etc.).

As an example, we read in Genesis 2:6: *"But there went up a mist from the earth, and watered the whole **face** (paniym) of the ground."* Using the word "person" in this passage would not make sense.

Some have attempted to use Psalms 17:15 as proof that the Hebrew writers understood God as a "person." *"As for me, I will behold thy face (paniym) in righteousness: I shall be satisfied, when I awake, with thy likeness."* A cursory reading of the text suggests that God may have been referred to here as a "person," as the word "paniym" can be translated as "person." However, when we read the rest of the passage: *"...when I awake, with thy likeness,"* we understand the correct intention of the inspired writer. The words "when I awake" refer to the Psalmist's resurrection. When he awakens, he is "satisfied ... with thy likeness". Young's Literal Translations has *"I--in righteousness, I see Thy face; I am satisfied, in awaking, with Thy form!"* The Psalmist will be satisfied to awaken with God's "form" or "image." What form would that be? A person? No, it will be "God's form." The apostle Paul tells us our resurrected bodies are no longer physical but spiritual bodies, like God: *"But some man will say, How are the dead raised up? and with what body do they come?" "So also, is the resurrection of the dead. It is sown in corruption; it is raised in incorruption: It is sown in dishonour; it is raised in glory: it is sown in weakness; it is raised in power: It is sown a natural body; it is raised a spiritual body. There is a natural body, and there is a spiritual body."* (1 Corinthians 15:35, 42-44).

The Word Coeternal in the Creed (s)

Coeternal: "adj. equally eternal, existing with something else eternally" (Oxford Dictionaries.com).

The word coeternal, as used in the Creeds, suggests that the Father, Son, and Holy Spirit have, individually, existed for eternity. Though the word "coeternal" is used in the creeds, the word "coeternal" cannot be found in the entire Bible. Eternal means "lasting or existing forever; without end or beginning." The word applies to God; God is eternal. But does it apply to the Son of God? It is an interesting fact that nowhere in the Bible is Jesus Christ called the "eternal Son." Nowhere. The Bible states that Jesus is the only "begotten Son," not the "eternal Son." Author and teacher Walter Martin addressed this question in his book titled "Kingdom of the Cults." I am indebted to him for the forthright way he treats this question of "eternal sonship." You will find his comments worthwhile: "Let us fix these things in our minds, then: (a) the doctrine of "eternal generation" or the eternal sonship of which springs from the Roman Catholic doctrine first conceived by Origin in A.D. 230, is a theory which opened the door theologically to the Arian and Sabellian heresies which today still plague the Christian Church in the realms of Christology." (b) The Scripture nowhere calls Jesus Christ the eternal Son of God, and He is never called Son at all prior to the incarnation, except in prophetic passages in the Old Testament." "The term 'Son' itself is a functional term, as is the term 'Father,' and has no meaning apart from time. The term "Father" incidentally never carries the descriptive adjective "eternal" in Scripture. Only the Spirit is called eternal (the eternal Spirit, Hebrews 9:14)" (7). In fairness, Martin is a well-respected Trinitarian. He defends the Trinitarian doctrine, except for the "eternal sonship." Martin correctly writes: "nowhere in the Bible does it say that Jesus is the 'eternal Son,' but it does say that He is the 'everlasting Father." Isaiah 9:6 *"For unto us a child is born, unto us a son is given: And the government shall be upon his shoulder: And his name shall be called Wonderful, Counseller, The mighty God, The everlasting Father, The Prince of Peace."* There is a significant difference between "eternal Son" and "everlasting Father." Jesus will not always, or eternally, be the Son. He will return to His former glory as the Almighty, eternal God. *"And now, O Father, glorify thou me **with thine own self** with the glory which I had with thee before the world was."*

The Messianic age began with the crucifixion of Jesus Christ. We learn through Paul's writings that this age will also end. When the end of the messianic age comes, the "manifestation" of God as the Son of God will no longer be necessary, since the age of grace will have ended. The Apostle Paul wrote the following regarding the ministry of the Son of God. *"Then cometh the end, when he shall have delivered up the kingdom to God, even the Father; when he shall have put down all rule and all authority and power. For he must reign till he hath put all enemies under his feet. The last enemy that shall be destroyed is death. For he hath put all things under his feet. But when he saith all things are put under him, it is manifest that he is excepted, which did put all things under him. And when all things shall be subdued unto him, then shall the Son also himself be subject unto him that put all things under him, that God may be all in all."* (1 Corinthians 15:24-28).

To aid us in understanding what this passage may mean, I offer the following quote from a respected Trinitarian source: i.e., the Pulpit Commentary. Here are author Adam Clarke's thoughts regarding verse 24: "When he shall have delivered up the kingdom to God. The kingdom delivered up is not that of the Coequal Godhead but the mediatorial kingdom. The divine kingdom 'shall not pass away.' (Daniel 7:13). But the mediatorial kingdom shall end in completion when the redemptive act has achieved its end." Continuing into verse 28, we read; "The Son also himself be subject: when the administration of the kingdom of grace is finally closed; when there shall be no longer any state of probation, and consequently no longer need of a distinction between the kingdom of grace and the kingdom of glory; **then the Son, as being man and Messiah, shall cease to exercise any distinct dominion; and God be all in all**: **There remaining no longer any distinction in the persons of the glorious Trinity,** as acting any distinct or separate parts in either the kingdom of grace or the kingdom of glory; and so the one infinite essence shall appear undivided and eternal." (emphasis mine). (8)

Clarke recognized that the ministry of the Son of God was not "eternal." In doing this, he acknowledges the fallacy of the "eternal sonship." (See also Matthew Henry, A Commentary on the Whole Bible, Vol. 6, page 589-590,

Ellicott's Commentary, Vol. 7, 8, Page 348 Zondervan, and The Biblical Illustrator Vol. 18, page 452, Baker).

Today, we are taught that the Godhead is an unexplainable mystery. Is it? While the Bible declares it a mystery: *"And without controversy great is the mystery of godliness: that **God was manifest in the flesh**, justified in the Spirit, seen of angels, preached unto the Gentiles, believed on in the world, received up into glory."* (1 Timothy 3:16), it is not "unexplainable." The Greek word for "mystery" is "musterion." It is a Greek word that means: "Primarily that which is known to the mustes, the initiated. (From muo; to initiate into mysteries) In the New Testament, it denotes not the mysterious or unknown (as with the English word) but that which is known only by divine revelation and is made known in a manner and at a time appointed by God and to those only who are illumined by His Spirit. In the ordinary sense, a mystery implies knowledge withheld; in its scriptural significance, it implies a truth revealed. Hence, the terms especially associated with the subject are "made known", "manifested", "revealed", "preached", "understood", and "dispensation". (9) The "mystery" is revealed, i.e., God was manifest in the flesh!

One further note regarding "eternal sonship." While the Son of God was described as the "only begotten," He is never described as the "eternal Son." Why? The words "only begotten" and "eternal" are opposites. The word "only begotten" in Greek is monogenes. It means "only begotten," "only," "only child." The word "eternal" in Greek is aiōnios: from (aion); perpetual (also used of a pastime, or past and future as well):- eternal, forever, everlasting, a world (began). One cannot be both begotten and eternal. Being begotten refers to a specific point in time. Being eternal means that one has always been " perpetual before time." Some may object by pointing out the promise to believers that, one day, we, too, will become eternal. That is correct; we will. However, the body we live in will not be the one that becomes "eternal." *"And as we have borne the image of the earthy, we shall also bear the image of the heavenly. Now this I say, brethren, that flesh and blood cannot inherit the kingdom of God; neither doth corruption inherit incorruption."* (1 Corinthians 15:49-50).

When the Athanasian Creed uses the word "co-equal," the Father, Son, and Holy Spirit are equal. The scriptures do not support this belief. Nowhere in scripture is Jesus called or described as "co-equal."

1. We know that Jesus, as the Son of God, was begotten and made a "little lower than the angels."

The Apostle Paul writes: *"But we see Jesus, who was made a little lower than the angels for the suffering of death, crowned with glory and honour; that he by the grace of God should taste death for every man."* (Hebrews 2:9).

2. Jesus, as a man, had limitations: *"Though he were a Son, yet learned he obedience by the things which he suffered..."* (Hebrews 5:8-9). In Luke's narrative, we learn that Jesus, as a child, "grew...." *"And the child grew, and waxed strong in spirit, filled with wisdom: and the grace of God was upon*

him." (Luke 2:40). We know that Jesus was tempted, tried, beaten, and bled. All of which speak to His humanity.

3. Jesus would die on the cross. *"When Jesus therefore had received the vinegar, he said, it is finished: and he bowed his head, and gave up the ghost."* (John 19:30). In what sense did God die at Calvary? Or the Holy Spirit? God cannot die; God, as the Spirit, cannot be crucified. It was the "man" Jesus Christ who died.

The manifestations of God are not coequal. We know that God was not "begotten"; Jesus was begotten. God does not have "limitations" and cannot "die." Jesus died! The same is true regarding God's Spirit. It was God manifest as Jesus that took on the "form of a servant": *"Let this mind be in you, which was also in Christ Jesus: Who, being in the form of God, thought it not robbery to be equal with God: But made himself of no reputation, and took upon him the form of a servant, and was made in the likeness of men: And being found in fashion as a man, he humbled himself and became obedient unto death, even the death of the cross."* (Philippians 2:6-8).

The prophet Isaiah holds the key to understanding the moment when God became a man. Here is what Isaiah wrote: *"For unto us a child is born, unto us a son is given: and the government shall be upon his shoulder: and his name shall be called Wonderful, Counsellor, The mighty God, The everlasting Father, The Prince of Peace."* (Isaiah 9:6) Notice the progression. First, a "child" is born. Then a "son" is "given." We know Jesus was "born," then "given" up to the cross. And we also read this "child," "son" is called "the mighty God, the everlasting Father."

If we understand that God became a man through the incarnation, we can understand the crucifixion of Jesus Christ. At this moment in history, the scriptures tell us that God becomes a man to meet the just demands of the law. *"And being found in fashion as a man, he humbled himself, and became obedient unto death, even the death of the cross."* (Philippians 2:8). We know the man as Jesus. He became the physical manifestation of the "invisible" God. *"In whom we have redemption through his blood, even the forgiveness of sins: Who is the image of the invisible God, the firstborn of every creature:"* (Colossians 1:14-15). God, as the Father, Jesus, and the Holy Spirit, are all manifestations of the one God. (See Appendix B) Though the word "coeternal" is used in the creeds, the word "coeternal" cannot be found in the entire Bible.

Footnotes Chapter 3

1. www.vatican/archive/ccc_css/archive/catechism/credo

2. Ibid

3. The Catholic Encyclopedia, The Athanasian Creed

4. John B. Noss, Man's Religion, MacMillan, 1974, page 453)

5. G.C.Storr & Flatt, Biblical Theo. S.S. Schumucker, Trans. 2nd ed.–Griffin, Wilcoxt C.

6. Barth, Karl. Church Dogmatics, Vol 1.1 Doctrine of the Word of God. Vol. 2. London: T & T Clark, 2010. Print. Study Edition. [351]

7. Martin, Walter. The Kingdom of the Cults, page 103 (Bethany Fellowship, 1977)

8. The Pulpit Commentary, Vol. 19, page 487 (Eerdmans 1950).

9. W.E. Vine, Expository Dictionary of New Testament Words, page 97

Chapter 4
The Trinity

"The truth that God is three and one is altogether a matter of faith; and in no way can it be demonstratively proved."
Thomas Aquinas

One would think they would readily find the doctrine of the Trinity, so central to the church, in the scriptures. However, neither the apostles (apostolic era 33 A.D.–90 A.D.) nor the post-apostolic leaders (90 A.D. to 140 A.D.) knew of or taught a trinity in relation to Jesus Christ. The first recorded use of the word "trinity" is the Greek word "tpias," used by Theophilus of Antioch ca. A.D. 180. Tpias was then translated into the Latin word Trinitas: "the number three, a triad, the Trinity." Tertullian, a Latin church father, used trinitas (160-230 A.D.). (1) By the next century, the word was widely used and could be found in the writings of Origen, a Greek writer, teacher, and church father. One of Origen's pupils was Gregory Thaumaturgus, who wrote the Exposition of the Faith between 260 and 270 A.D. In it he concludes: "There is therefore nothing created, nothing greater or less (literally, nothing subject) in the Trinity (oute oun ktiston ti, he doulon en te triadi), nothing superadded, as though it had not existed before, but never been without the Son, nor the Son without the Spirit; and this same Trinity is immutable and unalterable forever." "Such a formula, stating clearly the distinction between the Persons in the Trinity, and emphasizing the eternity, equality, immortality, and perfection, not only of the Father, but of the Son and of the

Holy Spirit, proclaims a marked advance on the theories of Origen." (wikipedia.org/wiki/Gregory Thaumaturgus)

At this time, the definition of the word Trinity was the state of being "threefold." However, some still taught that Jesus Christ was not divine, only a man. Among them were Theodotus of Byzantium in the second century and Dionysius, Bishop of Alexandria, in the middle of the third century. Others believed God created Jesus Christ; therefore, He was divine, but not God. While others believed Jesus Christ was God manifest in the flesh. With this background, we find ourselves at the Council of Nicaea in 325 A.D. Nicaea was an ancient city in the Byzantine Empire, now in northwestern Turkey. Emperor Constantine called together 300 bishops of the Christian church to formulate a creed, a statement of faith, which he hoped would end the Arian heresy that taught Jesus was not God and solidify his empire.

The Council of Nicaea became the official forum for the debate over contemporary and traditional views of Jesus Christ. During the two months that followed, the primary question was once again, "Who is Jesus Christ and what is his relationship to the Father?" Two men of dominance stood out during the council, each representing the two major doctrinal platforms of that time. Following in the footsteps of Theodotus of Byzantium and Dionysius, Arius denied the deity of Jesus Christ. Athanasius argued that the deity of Jesus Christ was absolute and unalterable.

It came down to two words: "homoiousios" (Arius), which meant "of like substance with the Father," or "homoousios" (Athanasius), which meant "of the same substance as the Father." While the difference may seem small, it was significant. If Jesus were only like the Father (homoiousios), Arius' view, but different from the Father, then Jesus' deity could not be supported. Athanasius prevailed, and they maintained Jesus' deity, at least for the present. However, as we read the Nicene Creed, we notice the council adopted the essence of what would become Trinitarian thought. While the creed does not use the word Trinity, the seeds of Trinitarianism were deeply planted. These "seeds" would blossom years later into the doctrine of the Trinity.

We know the early church continued to struggle with the question of Jesus Christ's deity and the Godhead. Eventually, they introduced words not found in the scriptures to describe the Godhead. Among the more important words were "person," "coequal," "coeternal," and "Trinity."

Chapter 5
The History of the Trinity

"Fourth-century Trinitarianism did not reflect accurately early Christian teaching regarding the nature of God; it was, on the contrary, a deviation from this teaching."
(The Encyclopedia Americana, p. 1956, p. 2941)

It is essential to know which leaders were more influential and what they believed about the Godhead. Following is a list of the most influential church leaders and their respective contributions to the creation of the Trinity.

Tertullian (ca. 155-ca. 240 A.D.)

Tertullian was the first to use the word Trinity (Latin trinitas). He also believed in "three persons, one substance." The "substance" he believed in "was a material substance that did not refer to a single God, but to the sharing of a portion of the substance of the Father (the only being who was fully God) with the Son and, through the Son, with the Holy Spirit." (1) Despite his use of the words "Trinity" and "persons," he believed in subordinationism, i.e., to consider Christ, as the Son of God, as inferior to the Father.

He became a follower of Montanism. This movement believed in "new prophecy," which referred to ecstatic utterances from oracles. They also held to an ascetic lifestyle, fasting and rejecting second marriages. He was eventually labeled a heretic and excommunicated.

Origen (ca. 184-253 AD)

Origen was a highly respected theologian in his day. His most noted works are the Hexapla, i.e., six translations of the Old Testament. He also wrote On First Principles, the first systematic work on Christian theology. He is reputed to have written between 2,000 and 6,000 works during his lifetime—a remarkable accomplishment. His teachings influenced both Athanasius and Arius. That is why both sides in the Arian conflict appealed to Origen's writings for support. Origen taught that Jesus was less than the Father in power, not in time. He believed the Father's deity was greater than the Son, as the Son had a beginning, i.e., eternal generation. Though Arius and Origen agreed on subordination within the Godhead, they disagreed on the question of the "eternal generation" of the Son. Arius believed Jesus was a created being, while Origen believed Jesus was "eternally generated."

Origen strongly opposed the Gnostic belief that Jesus came to Earth as a spirit rather than in human form. Origen believed Jesus took on a human body and soul. Some of Origen's beliefs were not popular, e.g., he believed in the pre-existence of souls and the "ransom theory" that espouses the death of Jesus Christ as a ransom paid to Satan for the souls of humanity. In 553 A.D., Emperor Justinian condemned him as a "heretic." He ordered his writings burned. At the Second Council of Constantinople (553 A.D.), some of his teachings were condemned as heretical. Some historians believe he was anathematized and condemned at this council.

Novatian (ca. 200–ca 257 A.D.)

Novation was an Anti-Pope being selected and consecrated by three Bishops. The Pope was Cornelius, who accused Novation of being possessed by Satan. (2) He and his followers refused to submit to the Pope. They did not believe a Christian who had committed idolatry or become an apostate could be forgiven and reunited with the church. Some historians believe they would accept them back if they were re-baptized. They were considered schismatics for rejecting the Pope and heretics for their stand on apostate Christians.

Tertullian, Origen, and Novatian made, perhaps, the most significant contributions to the emerging doctrine of the Trinity. Tertullian gave us the word Trinitas (Latin), which, translated into English, is our word "Trinity." Tertullian also believed and taught that God was three "persons." Origen is believed to have contributed to the idea of the "eternal generation" of the Son, while Novatian's contribution was his belief that the third person in the Godhead was the Holy Spirit. Origen and Novatian were later excommunicated in a twist of fate, while Tertullian would be labeled a heretic.

Arius (ca. 256-336 AD)

Arius was an ascetic and priest in Alexandria, Egypt. He believed: "If the Father begat the Son, he that was begotten had a beginning of existence: and from this, it is evident that there was a time when the Son was not. It, therefore, follows that he [the Son] had his substance from nothing." (Socrates Scholasticus, a fifth-century historian). According to Socrates, Arius believed the Son had a "beginning" and was not "eternal." This belief was to become known as "subordination," i.e., the Son of God was subordinate to the Father. Because of his belief in the nature of Jesus Christ and the Godhead, he and his teachings created a conflict among the church leaders. This conflict became the focus of the First Council of Nicaea.

Athanasius (ca. 296-373 A.D.)

Athanasius is also known as "Athanasius the Great" and "Athanasius the Confessor." He hailed from Alexandria, as did Arius and Origen. He became one of the most vigorous opponents of Arianism and a supporter of Trinitarianism at the Council of Nicaea. In 328 A.D., he became a Bishop. He devoted himself to defending the doctrine of the Trinity. He also endured five exiles, earning him the nickname "Athanasius Contra Mundum," meaning "Athanasius Against the World."

Footnotes Chapter 5

1. History of Trinitarian Doctrines. The Stanford Encyclopedia of Philosophy. Stanford University. Tuggy, Dale & Zalta, Edward N. (ed.) 2016

2. The Cyclopedia of Biblical, Theological, and Ecclesiastical Literature. New York: Harper and Brothers.

Chapter 6
Is Jesus Christ God or "a god?"

"But there were false prophets also among the people, even as there shall be false teachers among you, who privily shall bring in damnable heresies, even denying the Lord that bought them and bring upon themselves swift destruction. And many shall follow their pernicious ways; by reason of whom the way of truth shall be evil spoken of."
(2 Peter 2:1-2).

Is Jesus Christ God? Or is Jesus Christ a "god?" I mentioned earlier that some religious groups do not believe Jesus Christ is God. They think Jesus is a god (lowercase). They arrive at their conclusion using methods that Hebrew and Greek scholars universally reject. They often change or import words not found in ancient manuscripts. The proper translation protocol requires the translator to exegete rather than eisegete. The difference between exegete and eisegete is important: "Eisegesis is best understood when contrasted with exegesis. Exegesis is the process of drawing out the meaning of a text by reading its author's context and discoverable meaning. Eisegesis occurs when a reader imposes their interpretation into and onto the text. As a result, exegesis is objective when used, while eisegesis is regarded as highly subjective." It is "... the process of interpreting a text or a portion of text in such a way that the process introduces one's own presuppositions, agendas or biases into and onto the text." [1]

Eisegesis is what some religious groups do when translating the scriptures. They do it to prove or support a belief they already hold. Interestingly, their primary objective is to diminish, alter, or eliminate passages that demonstrate Jesus Christ's deity. To illustrate this practice, I have chosen an organization that engages in eisegeses when translating the Scriptures, the Jehovah's Witnesses. I chose this religious group for several reasons. First, they represent what many religious groups that deny the deity of Jesus Christ believe. Second, I chose them because of their numbers and aggressive proselytizing. (Unless otherwise noted, all scriptures in this section come from the Jehovah's Witnesses Bible, The New World Translation of the Holy Scriptures).

The Witnesses believe "Jesus and Jehovah God are not the same. Jesus is not equal to God." (2) They state that Jesus Christ is "a god" and not "the God." They use John 1:1 (among other Scriptures) to support their belief that Jesus is not God: *"Originally the Word was, and the Word was with God, and the Word was a god."* (John 1:1 NWT). The Witnesses justify this translation by stating there is a difference between the Greek words "theos" (god) without the article (the) and "theos" with the article (the God). When theos appears in scripture, without the article "the" before it, they believe it must be translated as "a god" or "god." In John 1:1, the article (the) does not precede the word Theos, so, following their reasoning, they translate it as "a god." However, in John chapter 1 of the New World Translation, theos appears without the article "the" six times: verses 1, 2,

6, 12, 13, and 18. Though theos appears six times, without the article "the" in the chapter, they only translate it as "a god" or "god" twice. In the remaining four cases, they translate theos without the article as 'God'. Why? Let's read the two verses where they translate "theos" as "a god": (vs. 1 and 18). Verse one reads: *"In the beginning was the Word, and the Word was with God (Theos), and the Word was a god (theos)."* Verse 18 reads: *"No man has seen God (Theos) at any time; the only-begotten **god** (huios) who is at the Father's side is the one who has explained Him."* These two passages demonstrate two things: first, they do not follow their translation guidelines. Their failure to follow their guidelines is glaringly apparent when we look at the appearance of the word "theos" in the Septuagint (the Greek Old Testament). The word "theos" appears 1343 times in the Septuagint. Of the 1343 times, the word theos appears 282 times without the article. However, the New World Translation translates it as "a god," "gods," or "godly" only 16 times. Following their guidelines, theos should have been rendered "god," "gods," "a god," or "godly" 282 times, not 16 times. Translating scripture demands uniformity and integrity. The Witnesses have an obvious bias against the deity of Jesus Christ.

Second, notice the addition of a word in verse 18: *"No man has seen God (Theos) at any time; the only-begotten **god** (huios) who is at the Father's side is the one who has explained Him."* They added "god" after the word "begotten." The word "god" is not in the original Greek text; the word "huios," for "son," is. This is another technique they use: adding words where they deem necessary to support their belief.

Returning to John 1:1, we discover another technique the Witnesses use in translating the scriptures, i.e., taking a scripture out of context. John 1:1 is an example: *"In the beginning was the Word, and the Word was with God, and the Word was **a god**. This one was in the beginning with God. All things came into existence through him, **and apart from him not even one thing came into existence.**"* (John 1:1-3, NWT). Read in isolation, this passage could support their belief that Jesus is "a god." However, reading the passage in context gives the reader a more precise understanding. *"In the beginning was the Word, and the Word was with God, and the Word was God. The same was in the beginning with God. **All things were made by him**; and without him was not any thing made that was made."* (KJV). Verse 3 tells the reader who the Word is; it is God the creator. Even their translation of verse 3 reads, *"and apart from him not even one thing came into existence,"* How could Jesus be both; a god and the creator God? Which is it? To bolster my argument that Jesus is the creator, I would offer the apostle Paul's view on who the creator is. Paul wrote; "*Who hath delivered us from the power of darkness, and hath translated us into the kingdom of his dear Son: In whom we have redemption through his blood, even the forgiveness of sins: Who is the image of the invisible God, the firstborn of every creature: For **by him were all things created**, that are in heaven, and that are in earth, visible and invisible, whether they be thrones, or dominions,* or principalities, or powers: **all things were created by him**, and for him: And he is before all things, and by him all things consist." (Colossians 1:13-17 KJV). The subject of this passage is Jesus Christ; therefore, Jesus Christ is the creator! If He is the creator, He is God.

The overwhelming number of translations render John 1:1 to mean "the word was God," not "a god. Here are a few: the King James version renders John 1:1-3: *"the Word was with God, and the Word was God...and apart from him not even one thing came into existence."* The English Greek N.T. has: *"And God was the Word."* The New English Bible has: *"What was, the Word was."* The Old English translation has "*God was the Word also.*"

The Witnesses also insist the words kurios (Lord) and Theos (God) in the New Testament should be translated as "Jehovah." However, they do not translate the words kurios or theos as Jehovah when kurios or theos refers to Jesus Christ. We find an example of this bias in Philippians 2:10-11: *"That at the name of Jesus every knee should bow, of things in heaven, and things in earth, and things under the earth; And that every tongue should confess that Jesus Christ is **Lord**, to the glory of God the Father."* (KJV) In this passage, Jesus is called Lord (kurios). However, the New World translators do not translate the word Lord (kurios) here as Jehovah: *"so that in the name of Jesus every knee should bend—of those in heaven and those on earth and those under the ground, and every tongue should openly acknowledge that Jesus Christ is Lord to the glory of God the Father."* (NWT.) They claim the reason for not translating "Lord" in this passage (and others) to "Jehovah" is because the word "Lord" is also applied to men, as when Sarah called Abraham Lord.

At first blush, their explanation sounds reasonable; it is true; some people in the Bible are called lord. But they have a problem with this passage as the quote also appears in Romans 14:11. When they translated Romans 14:11, they did use the word Jehovah where Lord appears: *"For it is written: "'As surely as I live,' says Jehovah, 'to me every knee will bend, and every tongue will make open acknowledgment to God."* (NWT) Why do they translate the word "Lord" into Jehovah in this verse but not in its companion verse, Philippians 2:10-11?

Perhaps the most blatant display of their bias occurs in John 20:28 when Thomas said to Jesus: "My Lord and my God" (NWT). Notice they did not translate "God" into the word "Jehovah." According to their rules of translation, it should have been. Some argue that Thomas was not speaking to Jesus when he exclaimed "my Lord and my God" but was crying out in joy to God in heaven. What does the scripture record? Thomas, "said unto **Him**...." Thomas was speaking to Jesus, not to the heavens. There are too many instances to list here where the translators of Jehovah's Witnesses have added, changed, and even deleted words to maintain their beliefs. I have attached them as Appendix D.

Sharp's Rule

Admittedly, there are verses in the Bible that appear to contradict the belief that Jesus Christ and God are one. But the shroud of mystery lifts considerably, thanks to Kenneth S. Wuest. Wuest, a professor of New Testament Greek, points out an essential rule of Greek grammar known as Sharp's rule. Granville Sharp was a Greek language scholar. He wrote: "When two nouns in the same case are connected by the Greek word 'and,' and the first noun is preceded by the article 'the,' and the second noun is not preceded by the article, the second noun refers to the same person or thing to which the first noun refers and is a further description of it. As an example, we read in Ephesians 4:11, *"And he gave some, apostles; and some, prophets; and some, evangelists; and some, pastors and teachers;"* the words "pastors" and "teachers" are in the same case and are connected by the word "and." The word "pastors" is preceded by the article 'the," whereas the word "teachers" is not. This construction requires us to understand that the words "pastors and teachers" refer to the same individual." [3] (The New International Version)

The significance of this rule becomes apparent when the words "God" and "Father" are in the same case and connected by the Greek word "and," while "God" is preceded by the article "the" and "Father" is not. The Greek word "and" can be translated by any of the following words: "and, even, also," depending upon the context in which they are found. Wuest then cites the following scriptures: Romans 15:6, I Corinthians 15:24, 2 Corinthians 1:3, 11:31,

Galatians 1:4, Ephesians 5:20, Philippians 4:20, I Thessalonians 1:3, 3:11, 13. These passages show that "God" and "Father" are the same. Wuest notes that " Father " further describes "God." For example, in 2 Peter 1:1, we read the expression "the (tou) God and our Savior Jesus Christ," and here the rule applies. (Note the English translations do not show the article "the," though it is in the Greek text.) Thus, "Savior Jesus Christ" is a further description of "the God." The cults overlook this grammatical rule as it provides compelling evidence that Jesus Christ is God. We see this again in Titus 2:13, which, according to Mr. Wuest, could be translated "the Great God "even" our Savior Jesus Christ." In the Bible, Jesus Christ is called "God" in many places; this is clear if you understand and apply Sharp's rule.

Footnotes Chapter 6

1. www.wikipedia.org/wiki/eisegesis

2. This Good News of the Kingdom, Watchtower Bible and Tract Society of Pa., 1965

3. Wuest, Word Studies in the Greek New Testament Vol. III, Treasures from the Greek New Testament, Greek Grammar and the Deity of Jesus Christ, page 31, Eerdmans

Chapter 7
God is One

"0 Lord of hosts, God of Israel, that dwellest between the cherubim thou art the God, even thou alone, of all the kingdoms of the earth: thou hast made heaven and earth."
(Isaiah 37:18)

One of the "pillars" of the Trinitarian doctrine is the belief that the Godhead comprises "three persons." Trinitarians believe this even though the Israelites distinguished themselves by their steadfast belief in monotheism, i.e., "one" God, not three persons. Perhaps the question before us should be, "What does the word 'one' in the Hebrew Old Testament mean?" How did the Jews understand the meaning of "one?"

In the Hebrew Old Testament, the word "one" appears many times. The problem is this: in Hebrew, "one" does not always mean an absolute one. It could mean one group or one bunch, not an absolute one. Some teach that "one" in this scripture: *"Hear, O Israel: The LORD our God is one LORD:"* (Deuteronomy 6:4), does not mean an absolute one. They believe the word "one" is plural in this passage and therefore refers to a plurality of persons in the Godhead. As support for this belief, some cite another verse: *"And God said, Let us make man in our image, after our likeness: and let them have dominion over the fish of the sea, and over the fowl of the air, and over the cattle, and over all the earth, and over every creeping thing that creepeth upon the earth."* (Gen. 1:26) To understand if this passage refers to God in the plural, read the following verse: *"So God created man in his own image, in the image of God created he him; male and female created he them."* (Genesis 1:27).

Some believe a plurality exists in verse 26 while remaining silent concerning verse 27. *"So God created man in his (singular) own image, in the image of God created he him (singular); male (singular) and female (singular) created he them (taken together, plural)."* God created man in His image, and there was only one (singular) man. Who was God speaking to in verse 26 when He said, "Let us (plural) make the man (singular) in our (plural) image"? The scriptures do not supply that answer. I offer five possible solutions to consider.

1. Himself.

2. An Angelic host -angels already existed; they were spirits, and God had talked to them on other occasions (Isaiah 6:8).

3. A plurality of Majesty. It is common for Kings and Potentates to speak in the plural while referring to themselves.

4. God may have been talking to the earth, as Adam was made of the dust of the earth, together with God's Spirit. God has spoken to the earth, the mountains, trees, rivers, etc., on other occasions.

5. We do not know.

So, which is it? Did the Jews believe God was an absolute "one," or did they believe there was a plurality of "three persons" in the Godhead?

Three Hebrew words have been used to support the Trinitarian view of three persons in the Godhead: Echad, Yahid, and Yachid. Understanding what these words mean and how they are applied in scripture is critical to one's understanding of how the Jews understood God to be one.

Echad

The Hebrew word for "one" is "echad," Strong's H259, occurring 952 times in 739 verses in the Hebrew concordance of the KJV. The KJV translates it: one (687x), first (36x), another (35x), other (30x), any (18x), once (13x), eleven (with H6240) (13x), every (10x), certain (9x), an (7x), some (7x), miscellaneous (87x).

The overwhelming use of the word echad is the cardinal number "one," occurring 687 times. The other use of echad is the word "first," occurring 36 times; it is an ordinal number denoting place: first place, second place, etc., not plurality. The difference is important; a cardinal number tells us how many of something there are (quantity), one, two, three, etc. An ordinal number does not indicate quantity. Ordinal numbers tell us the place or position of something: first place, second place, third, etc. (echad may also mean "single," e.g., "one house" e.g., *"In one house shall it be eaten; thou shalt not carry forth ought of the flesh abroad out of the house; neither shall ye break a bone thereof"* (Exodus 12:46, see also Exodus 37:22, Numbers 13:23, 1 Kings 8:56, Isaiah 51:2, Zechariah 3:9). Is echad ever translated as a 'compound unity, as some suggest?

Trinitarians believe the word "echad" ([achat; feminine]), in Hebrew, is a "proof" for a "compound unity" or being one of a "group of members" in referring to God in the Old Testament. How can a person determine how it is to be understood? The text in which the word "echad" is found often determines whether it is a cardinal number, one, alone, an ordinal number, or as a compound unit, i.e., one group with many members. One thing is clear: echad does not always mean 'one of many' or 'one of a group' or 'one of a cluster'. I have already noted that the overwhelming use of the word echad is the cardinal number one.

Some conclude that echad is used in the Old Testament to mean a compound unity, i.e., one group with multiple members: like the "one cluster of grapes" (Numbers 13:23). From this scripture, they deduce God must also be a compound unity when the word echad is used to describe God. Following this logic, they believe the use of the word echad in Numbers 13:23 proves a plurality of persons in the Godhead existed in the Old Testament. Is this assumption correct? Here is the passage in question: *"And they came unto the brook of Eshcol and cut down from thence a branch with **one (echad)** cluster of grapes, and they bare it between two upon a staff, and they brought of the pomegranates, and of the figs."* (Numbers 13:23).

Some insist that echad, in Numbers 13:23, refers to a "compound unity," i.e., a "cluster of grapes." Does "one cluster of grapes" refer to a "compound unity" or "one" (single item) cluster of grapes? Two words in the quote need to be examined: "one" and "cluster." The word "one" we know is "echad." We also know that this word is most often used to denote cardinal numbers, such as 1, 2, 3, etc. Does this passage mean "one" or a "compound unity"? The answer lies in the word "cluster."

While we may debate the proper use of echad in this passage, the word "cluster" is beyond debate. The Hebrew word translated as a "cluster" is "Eshkol." Strong's Greek and Hebrew Dictionary reads "… a bunch of grapes or other fruit.…" This Hebrew word is rendered, in the scriptures, as "cluster" eight times and a "cluster of grapes" (in this passage) once. If echad meant a "compound unity" and Eshkol meant "a cluster of grapes," that would be redundant. It would not make any sense. If, however, we understand the word "echad" to mean "one," then the passage makes sense, as it would tell us they had "one," single, "cluster of grapes," not "one compound unity" of a "cluster of grapes."

The attempt to draw an inference that echad (one) could mean a "unity" or "compound unity," and therefore, the use of the word "one" in referring to God could also refer to a "unity" or "compound unity," is incorrect. A Hebrew translation of the passage is: *"They cut down a branch with a single cluster of grapes [eshkol anavim echad].* (Numbers 13:23). We see another example of echad used in Genesis 2:24 to denote the cardinal number one: *"Therefore shall a man leave his father and his mother and shall cleave unto his wife: and they shall be one (echad) flesh."* While Adam and Eve have become "one" flesh, they remain two, separate people. There is no "compound unity" of persons here.

In Genesis 11:1, we see echad being used, again, as a cardinal number: *"And the whole earth was of one (echad) language, and of one speech."* The use of the word one in this passage is the cardinal one: *"Go to, let us go down, and there confound their language, that they may not understand one another's speech."* We know that is correct; else, why confound their language?

The Jewish Shema reads: *"Hear O Israel, the Lord is our God; the Lord is one (echad). And as for you, you shall love the Lord your God with all your heart, with all your soul, and with all your strength."* The Shema is the Jew's expression of their foundational belief in one God. Looking at the word "echad" as a "compound unity" or a member of a "group" would twist the Jewish Shema beyond recognition. Using this logic, the Shema would read: "Hear, O Israel: The Lord our God, the Lord is a 'unity' or "compound unity." Or, according to some, it may be read, "Hear O Israel, The Lord our God, the Lord, is a member of a group." How would this distinguish the God of Israel from all the pagan gods? How could the God of Israel be the "only" God of the Jews if their God was a compound unity or a member of a group?

Yāchîd

The second Hebrew word Yāchîd is "only"; it is Strong's 3173, yachid (yahid), occurring 12 times in the Hebrew concordance of the KJV. It is translated as: only (6), darling (2), only child (1), only son (1), desolate (1), and solitary (1). (Strong's Talking Greek & Hebrew Dictionary).

Trinitarians who believe echad could mean a "compound unity" or a "plurality," and thus support the belief of three persons in the Godhead, appeal to the use of this word yachid. Trinitarian's reason is that if the writer of Numbers 13:23 wanted to convey an absolute "one," "only one," a "single," instead of a "compound unity," the writer would have used the Hebrew word "yachid" instead of "echad,"; as yachid may mean "... only, only one, solitary." They base this belief upon a faulty assumption. They believe yachid is to be understood as a cardinal number: 1,2, e.g., "only one," "one," "alone." The scriptures do not support this assumption. Yachid does not mean the cardinal number "one." As an example, we read in Genesis 22:2: *"And he said, Take now thy son, thine only son Isaac, whom thou lovest, and get thee into the land of Moriah; and offer him there for a burnt offering upon one of the mountains which I will tell thee of."* Notice the use of the word "only" in this passage. It is the word "yachid" in Hebrew. God calls Isaac, Abraham's "only (yachid) son." Isaac is not Abraham's only (one) son. Isaac has an older brother Ishmael. How then is Isaac "yachid"? He is not the "only one" nor is he "alone" or "solitary." The word "yachid" here would mean "unique" and not "only" or "solitary." (see Brown-Driver-Briggs Hebrew definitions).

Isaac was yachid, "unique," different from his brother Ishmael in that he was the son of promise. Still, Isaac was not the "only" son. It should be noted that the word "son" is in italics in the scriptures; this tells the reader it is not in the Hebrew text. The passage reads, "… thine only Isaac…." Here, yachid denotes a "quality," not a "quantity." Isaac was unique but not the "only one." Any attempt to use the word yahid to show a "compound unity" in the Godhead is futile. Yachid doesn't mean a "compound unity" or "plurality."

The word yachid is used only 12 times in the scriptures; 7 times, it refers to an "only" or unique "child." If the writer of Numbers 13:23 had used yachid (unique) instead of echad (cardinal number), all the reader would have known is that the cluster of grapes was "unique" in some way. It turns out the cluster was unique. It took two men to carry it! Its size is what would have been unique: the "only one," "alone," and "solitary." Remember, echad, the word used in Numbers 13:23, is a cardinal number. It tells the reader that the "number" of clusters he is referring to is one cluster, not two, three, or more.

Yāchad

There is a third Hebrew word for "unity" or "community." It is yachad. It is Strong's 3161 occurring three times in the Old Testament: unite (2), join (1). It comes from a "primitive root; to be (or become) one; join, unite." (Strong's Talking Greek & Hebrew Dictionary). Yachad is the Hebrew word that would denote "unity" or "community, not echad. We find yachad in the Dead Sea Scrolls. A "group of priests and their disciples" at Qumran are called "The Yachad: The Union, the Comm-unity." This discovery sheds additional light on the correct meaning of yachad. Yachad appears three times in the Old Testament. The word was used in the scriptures to denote unity of "mind," "will," or sharing things in common, i.e., a "community."

Genesis 49:6 *"O my soul, come not thou into their secret; unto their assembly, mine honour, be not thou **united:** for in their anger they slew a man, and in their self-will they digged down a wall."* Here we read Jacob's lament over his sons and tells his "soul" not to become like them.

Psalms 86:11 *"Teach me thy way, O LORD; I will walk in thy truth: **unite** my heart to fear thy name."* This suggests a union of "will" or "purpose."

Isaiah 14:20, *"Thou shalt not be **joined** with them in burial, because thou hast destroyed thy land, and slain thy people: the seed of evildoers shall never be renowned."* The prophet tells the King of Babylon that he will not be buried with his people in death.

Though this word, not echad, is the proper word to denote joining or unity, it is not used in Numbers 13:23 to describe the cluster of grapes as "one." More importantly,

yachad is never used to describe God. The emphasis in the Old Testament was not on God's uniqueness but His "oneness." In contrast to the many gods of the pagans, Israel served and worshipped one God. The pagans had "unique" gods and goddesses, too. Israel had one God, the true God. "Hear, O Israel! The LORD is our God, the LORD alone." (International Standard Version, Deuteronomy 6:4).

The Number One

In the New Testament, the Greek word for "one" is "heis." It is Strong's 1520 occurring in the New Testament 272 times: one (229x), "a" (9x), other (6x), some (6x), not translated (4x), miscellaneous (18x).

In Vines Expository Dictionary of New Testament Words, we read: "One. A. Numeral: "HEIS, the first cardinal numeral, masculine (feminine and neuter nominative forms are mia and hen, respectively)" Vine's states the Greek word HEIS "is used to signify (I) (a) one in contrast to many... or a cardinal number one." Vine's also points out the word "one" has been used "emphatically," i.e., "a single one to the exclusion of others... (c) "one and the same," e.g., Romans 3:30, RV, "God is one," i.e., there is not "one" God for the Jew and one for the Gentile..." And Vine's states some uses of the word "one" are "metaphoric" (b) metaphorically, union and concord..." (1)

Here is an example of the word one (heis) as a cardinal number: *"And unto one he gave five talents, to another two, and to another one; to every man according to his several ability; and straightway took his journey."* (Matthew 25:15) Here the intent is evident, in distributing the "talents," He gave "to another one." One (heis) is used metaphorically in Philippians 1:27 *"Only let your conversation be as it becometh the gospel of Christ: that whether I come and see you, or else be absent, I may hear of your affairs, that ye stand fast in one (heis) spirit, with one (mia) mind striving together for the faith of the gospel..."* The words "one spirit" and "one mind" are metaphoric.

There are instances in which the word is used to denote "unity" or "union." Here is an example: *"There is neither Jew nor Greek, there is neither bond nor free, there is neither male nor female: for ye are all one in Christ Jesus."* (Galatians 3:28). In this passage, the word "one" is being used to express our "unity" or "oneness" in Christ. But the unity here is not a unity of "persons" but a unity of "purpose." When a believer becomes "one" with Christ, they are acting out of a sense of purpose. This same thought is found in John 10:30, "I and my Father are one." The word for "one" in the text is "hen," not "heis." The Greek word hen is the neuter form of "one," while the word "heis" is the masculine form. The difference is essential. By using the neuter form of the word "hen" in John 10:30, the writer tells the reader that Jesus and the Father are "one in purpose or will." In John 17:21,22, Jesus prayed: *"That they (His disciples) may all be one,"* and He added, *"that they may be one even as we are one."* John used the same Greek word (hen) for "one" in both instances. Clearly, Jesus' disciples were not part of the Trinity. They share a oneness of purpose and will with the Father and the Son, the same oneness that unites God and Christ Jesus. Young's Concise Critical Bible Commentary gives us further insight: "The particle en [hen] being of the neuter gender, can hardly signify 'one being, i.e., one God,' but rather "one in will, purpose, counsel..." (2) The scriptures are clear in this; there is only one "person" in the Godhead, Jesus Christ. God became a person, a human, in the incarnation. Jesus taught that God was Spirit (John 4:24), not a separate person.

Monos

Strong's Number 3441 (monos) occurs in the New Testament 47 times: only (24x), alone (21x), by (one's) self (2x).

In the New Testament, three passages refer to God as "monos," the "only" God, or potentate. The apostle Paul wrote the first passage: *"Now unto the King eternal, immortal, invisible, the only (monos) wise God, be honour and glory for ever and ever. Amen."* (1 Timothy 1:17). Here, Paul is telling the reader there is "only" one (monos) God; "... the only wise God...." It is impossible to interpret this to suggest a trinity.

The second occurrence of monos is in Jude's letter: *"To the only (monos) wise God **our Saviour**, be glory and majesty, dominion and power, both now and ever. Amen."* (Jude 1:25). Jude also recognizes God as a "monos" or "only" wise God. There is only one "wise God and Saviour" for Jude and Paul. Jude gives the reader a "clue" as to "who" the "only wise God" is; He is "our Saviour." Luke reveals who the Savior is: *"For unto you is born this day in the city of David a Saviour, which is Christ the Lord."* (Luke 2:11). Jesus Christ is our Savior. John, the apostle, also acknowledged Jesus as the Saviour: *"And said unto the woman, Now we believe, not because of thy saying: for we have heard him ourselves, and know that this is indeed the Christ, the Saviour of the world."* (John 4:42). (See also 1 Timothy 2:3, 2 Timothy 1:10, Titus 1:4, Titus 2:13).

Paul, writing to Timothy, penned these words: *"Which in his times he shall shew, who is the blessed and **only Potentate, the King of kings, and Lord of lords**; Who only hath immortality, dwelling in the light which no man can approach unto; whom no man hath seen, nor can see: to whom be honour and power everlasting. Amen."* (1 Timothy 6:15). The question is, "who" are Paul and Jude referring to as the "only" wise God, the "only Potentate, the King of Kings, and Lord of Lords;"? We find the unambiguous answer in the Revelation: *"These shall make war with the Lamb, and the Lamb shall overcome them: for he is Lord of lords, and King of kings: and they that are with him are called, and chosen, and faithful."* (Revelation 14:4). Jesus is the "Lord of Lords and King of Kings." (see also Revelation 5:6). The use of the word "lamb" in Revelation 14:4 is a metaphor for Jesus. He is the lamb. We know this is correct as John the Baptizer called Jesus the "lamb" of God: *"The next day John seeth Jesus coming unto him, and saith, Behold the Lamb of God, which taketh away the sin of the world."* (John 1:29, also see vs. 36).

Two other passages have the word "monos" in them. They appear to suggest a "plurality" as they mention both God and the Lord Jesus Christ in each passage: *"And this is life eternal, that they might know thee the only (monos) true God, and Jesus Christ, whom thou hast sent."* (John 17:3), and *"For there are certain men crept in unawares, who were before of old ordained to this condemnation, ungodly men, turning the grace of our God into lasciviousness, and denying the only (monos) Lord God, and our Lord Jesus Christ."* (Jude 1:4).

Using the word "monos" in describing "the only true God" and "Lord God" tells us the writer believed God is "one," "only," or "alone." Some, however, believe these passages show a "plurality" or two persons in the Godhead: 1. the "only true God," "Lord God," and 2. "Jesus Christ," or "our Lord Jesus Christ." Is this interpretation correct? No, not according to Sharp's rule (see chapter 6). I will restate it here: "when two nouns in the same case are connected by the Greek word "and," and the first noun is preceded by the article "the," and the second noun is not preceded by the article, the second noun refers to the same person or thing to which the first noun refers, and is a further description of it. For instance, the words "pastors" and "teachers" in Ephesians 4:11 are in the same case and are connected by the word "and." The word "pastors," is preceded by the article "the," whereas the word "teachers" is not. This construction requires us to understand that the words "pastors and teachers" refer to the same individual." (3) (the New International Version)

Titus 2:13 is an example of how the rule is applied: *"Looking for that blessed hope, and the glorious appearing of the great God and our Saviour Jesus Christ."* Sharp's rule applies here as the word "God" is preceded by the article "the," and the word connects the two nouns "and," and the second noun, "Savior," does not have an article "the" preceding it. Following the rule, "the great God" and "Saviour Jesus Christ" refer to the same person, not two. I would also add that "appearing" (epiphaneia) is always and only applied to Jesus Christ in the New Testament. (See Timothy 6:14, 2 Timothy 1:10, 4:1, 4:8, and 1 Peter 1:7).

2 Peter 1:1 is another example of Sharp's rule: *"Simon Peter, a servant and an apostle of Jesus Christ, to them that have obtained like precious faith with us through the righteousness of God and our Saviour Jesus Christ:"* Young's Literal Translation renders it: *"Simeon Peter, a servant and an apostle of Jesus Christ, to those who did obtain a like precious faith with us in the righteousness of our God and Saviour Jesus Christ:"* Some argue Sharp's rule does not apply in 2 Peter 1:1 as the article "the" does not appear before the word "God." Those who disagree must explain 2 Peter 1:11: *"For so an entrance shall be ministered unto you abundantly into the everlasting kingdom of our Lord and Saviour Jesus Christ."* This passage contains the "identical construction" found in 2 Peter 1:1. The difference is that, in verse 1, Peter uses the word "Theos" (God); in verse 11, he uses the word "Kurio" (Lord). We know in verse 11 that the translation "Lord and Saviour" refers to Jesus Christ. If Jesus Christ is "Lord and Saviour," then,

logically, He is also "God and Saviour." (see also 1 Peter 2:20, 3:2, 3:18).

The Godhead is in Jesus Christ

When I speak of the "Godhead," I refer to God's three primary manifestations (modes): the Father, Son, and Holy Spirit. In the apostle Paul's letter to the Colossians, he uses the word Godhead when he writes: *"For in him dwelleth all the fulness of the Godhead bodily."* (Colossians 2:9). Young's Literal Translation has *"because in him doth tabernacle all the fulness of the Godhead bodily."* If this is true, and it must be true, we need to ask, "How" is the Godhead in Jesus Christ?

Let's begin with a question: Is Jesus called the Father in scripture? Yes. He is identified as the Father in Isaiah 9:6: *"For unto us a child is born, unto us a son is given. And his name shall be called wonderful, counselor, the mighty God, the everlasting Father."* Based on the text, we know the prophet was speaking about Jesus. We read, "... a child is born. " This refers to the birth of Jesus. Then the prophet writes, "... a son is given". We know that the "son of God" was "given" at the crucifixion. The prophet identifies this "child," this "son," as *"wonderful, counselor, the mighty God, the everlasting Father."* This is the only place in scripture where the Father is called "everlasting, " and it applies to the "child" and "son," i.e., Jesus Christ.

Did Jesus ever claim He was the Father? Yes. In John, the 14th chapter, Jesus speaks to the apostles, explaining that He is going to be crucified and go away for a brief time (3 days) and return: *"... ye believe in God, believe also in me. In my Father's house are many mansions; if it were not so, I would have told you. I go to prepare a place for you. And if I go and prepare a place for you, I will come again, and receive you unto myself; that where I am, there ye may be also. And whither I go ye know, and the way ye know. Thomas saith unto him, Lord, we know not whither thou goest; and how can we know the way? Jesus saith unto him, I am the way, the truth, and the life: no man cometh unto the Father, but by me.* **If ye had known me, ye should have known my Father also: and from henceforth ye know him and have seen him.** *Philip saith unto him, Lord, shew us the Father, and it sufficeth us. Jesus saith unto him,* **Have I been so long time with you, and yet hast thou not known me, Phillip? He that hath seen me hath seen the Father;** *and how sayest though then, shew us the Father? Believest thou not that I am in the Father, and the Father in me? the words that I speak unto you I speak not of myself: but the Father that dwelleth in me, he doeth the works. Believe me that I am in the Father, and the Father in me: or else believe me for the very works' sake. Verily, verily, I say unto you, He that believeth on me, the works that I do shall he do also; and greater works than these shall he do; because I go unto my Father."* (John 14:1-11).

Jesus said: "He that hath seen me hath seen the Father." Phillip was confused, so Philip asked, *"Lord, show us the father, and it will be sufficient."* Jesus answered, "Philip have I been so long time with you, and yet thou hast *not known me? He that hath seen me hath seen the father. How can you say show us the father?"* Jesus Christ claimed to be the Father. This claim is in harmony with the prophet Isaiah. Isaiah called the "son" the "everlasting father" (Isaiah 9:6). The identity of the Father is especially important for believers as the Bible states emphatically that only the Father is God: *"But to us there is but one God, the Father, of whom are all things, and we in Him, and one Lord Jesus Christ, by whom are all things, and we by Him."* (1Corinthians 8:6).

Is Jesus Christ referred to as the Holy Spirit? Yes. If Jesus is not the Holy Spirit, then how do we explain or understand the following scriptures? *"To whom God would make known what the riches of the glory of this mystery among the Gentiles is; which is Christ in you, the hope of glory."* (Colossians 1:27). How is it that Christ is "in" us? By His Spirit, that is how. The following scriptures also reveal that Jesus Christ is referred to as the Holy Spirit: *"And because ye are sons, God hath sent forth the Spirit of his Son into your hearts crying, Abba, Father."* (Galatians 4:6). Again, we read: *"For I know that this shall turn to my salvation through your prayer, and the supply of the Spirit of Jesus Christ"* (Philippians 1:19). Peter wrote: *"Searching what, or what manner of time **the Spirit of Christ** which was in them did signify, when it testified beforehand the sufferings of Christ, and the glory that should follow."* (1 Peter 1:11).

To further understand how Jesus and the Holy Spirit are one, we read: *"And I will pray the Father, and he shall give you another Comforter, that he may abide with you forever; even the Spirit of truth; whom the world cannot receive, because it seeth him not, neither knoweth him: but ye know him; for he dwelleth with you, and shall be in you."* (John 14:17). Note that Jesus told them, "you know him for he dwelleth with you" and "shall be in you." It was Jesus whom they knew and who was dwelling with them. In the following passage, Jesus spoke of the Father sending another comforter, even the "spirit of truth." Jesus claimed to be "the truth" ... "I am the way, the truth, and the life...." If Jesus claimed to be the "truth" (and He is), then the "Spirit of truth" must be His spirit.

In verse 18, we discover another exciting insight into Jesus' complete identity: *"I will not leave you comfortless, I will come to you."* First, I would ask the reader to notice the word "comfortless" in the text. Jesus says He will not leave them "comfortless." The word "comfortless" is orphanos in Greek. From this word, we get the English word "orphans". Another way to render this word could be "parentless" or "fatherless." Jesus said He would not leave them fatherless. Darby's Translation reads: *"I will not leave you, orphans. I am coming to you."* Many other expositors agree that Jesus told them He would not leave them "orphans" or "fatherless." (see Ellicott's Commentary, Meyer's NT Commentary, Cambridge Bible for Schools and colleges, Pulpit Commentary, Barnes' Notes on the Bible, Matthew Henry's Concise Commentary, Jamieson-Fausset-Brown Bible Commentary, etc.) Returning to the passage, notice what He said, "I will come to you." Here, Jesus Christ plainly identifies the Holy Spirit as His Spirit, saying, "I will come to you." In verse 26, we read: *"But the comforter, which is the Holy Ghost, whom the Father will send in my name ..."* In what name does the Holy Spirit come? Jesus said the Holy Spirit would come in "His" name: *"But the Comforter, which is the Holy Ghost, whom the Father will send in my name, he shall teach you all things, and bring all things to your remembrance, whatsoever I have said unto you."* (John 14:26).

Footnotes Chapter 7

1. Vine's Expository Dictionary of Biblical Words, New Testament Section, pg. 446

2. Young's Concise Critical Bible Commentary, p. 62, Baker Book House, 1977

3. Wuest, Word Studies in the Greek New Testament Vol. III, Treasures from the Greek New Testament, Greek Grammar and the Deity of Jesus Christ, page 31, Eerdmans

Chapter 8
Father, Son, and Holy Spirit

"I Jesus have sent mine angel to testify unto you these things in the churches. I am the root and the offspring of David, and the bright and morning star." (Revelation 22:16).

In this chapter, I will examine the words "Father," "Son," and "Holy Spirit" in their original languages, i.e., Hebrew and Greek.

The Father

In the passage above, we encounter a paradox. Jesus claims to be both the "root" and "the offspring" of David. How can that be? The Trinitarian doctrine cannot adequately explain this passage. The answer to this apparent paradox lies in correctly understanding the words "Father, Son, and Holy Spirit" as they appear in the scriptures. The word "Father" suggests a male, a person. When we read the words "father" and "son," it is natural to think of the Father and the Son as two persons. However, Jesus taught that God was Spirit (John 4:24), not a person. This is important. Even Moses understood God was not a person. He wrote, *"God is not a man,"* (a person) *"that he should lie; neither the son of man, that he should repent: hath he said, and shall he not do it? or hath he spoken, and shall he not make it good?"* (Numbers 23:19). God is Spirit. The word "father" refers to a characteristic, attribute or manifestation of God as a father to His children (see notes on "comfortless" above).

Using the word Father to refer to God in the Old Testament is relatively rare; by some counts, it occurs only 15 times. The word Father is used metaphorically when referring to God in the Old Testament. In the New Testament, the word Father appears numerous times. However, the Trinitarian phrase "God the Father" is never used. This phrase appears nowhere in the Bible. Neither does "God the Son" nor "God the Holy Spirit."

Interestingly, Jesus is known as the Father in the Old and New Testaments. We find it in the writings of the prophet Isaiah; *"For unto us a child is born, unto us a son is given: and the government shall be upon his shoulder: and his name shall be called Wonderful, Counsellor, The mighty God, The everlasting Father, The Prince of Peace."* (Isaiah 9:6). This passage is unique in this regard, it is the only time the Father is called "everlasting," and it refers to Jesus, who, we know, is the "child" and "son" in the passage. Here, in Isaiah 9:6, we find a similar paradox to that in Revelation 22:16: the son (offspring) is also the Father (root).

The apostle John records a conversation between Jesus and a disciple named Phillip. Here is part of the exchange between them: *"Jesus saith unto him, I am the way, the truth, and the life: no man cometh unto the Father, but by me. If ye had known me, ye should have known my Father also: and from henceforth ye know him and have seen him. Philip saith unto him, Lord, shew us the Father, and it sufficeth us."* (John 14:6-8). Jesus told Philip, *"henceforth you know Him and have seen Him...."* Phillip replies, *"Lord, shew us the Father, and it sufficeth us."* Jesus *answers Phillip, "Have I been so long a time with you and yet hast thou not known me, Philip? He that hath seen me hath seen the Father."* (John 14:9). Jesus Christ told Phillip, if you have seen me, you have seen the Father. How can this be if the Father and the Son were two "separate persons"? Jesus claimed to be one with the Father, not two beings, separate, independent of each other, but one (John 10:30). According to the apostle John, the world did not know the Father; *"Behold, what manner of love the Father hath bestowed upon us, that we should be called the sons of God: therefore the world knoweth us not, because it knew him not."* (1 John 3:1). The only way the world could see or know the Father was through knowing Jesus Christ.

The Son

It appears there may be a conflict in the phrases "The Son of God" and 'The Son of Man. One, the Son of God, suggests deity, while the other, the Son of Man, suggests humanity. Taken together, they reveal Jesus' dual nature as God and man. First, we read of Jesus' humanness: He hungered (Matthew 4:2), He slept (Matthew 8:24), He wearied (John 4:6), He wept (John 11:35), and He died (1 Corinthians 15:3), all as a man. Yet He was God in all the fullness: *"For in him dwelleth all the fulness of the Godhead bodily."* (Colossians 2:9). Second, we read that he possessed qualities that belong only to God, i.e., Jesus is the Creator of the world (Colossians 1:16), Saviour of humankind (Luke 2:11, Isaiah 43:11). He forgives sin (Mark 2:5-7), and He is worshipped (Hebrew 1:6, Deuteronomy 20:3-5). This list is not exhaustive; it merely represents some scriptures in which Jesus Christ is recognized as God. Now, let us take a closer look at the titles themselves to determine their true meaning in the original Greek of the New Testament.

The Son of God

This phrase confuses some people because they immediately form a mental picture of a father (the greater) and his son (the lesser). The question is, how is this phrase applied to Jesus? The Greek word for Son is "Huios." Huios is used in the scriptures as 1. the relation of a male offspring to a parent, 2. metaphorically of the character or nature of something.

A Greek word study tells us when "huios" (son) is used regarding Jesus; it does not refer to the more restricted meaning of a male offspring to a father. Instead, Jesus is called the "huios" of God because he is the "express image" of the character and nature of God: *"God, who at sundry times and in divers manners spake in time past unto the fathers by the prophets, Hath in these last days spoken unto us by his Son, whom he hath appointed heir of all things, by whom also he made the worlds; Who being the brightness of his glory, and the express image of his person, and upholding all things by the word of his power, when he had by himself purged our sins, sat down on the right hand of the Majesty on high;...."* (Hebrews 1:1-3).

W. E. Vine writes "Son": "That is to say, the Son of God... is not so entitled because He at any time began to derive His being from the father but because He is and ever has been the expression of what the Father is." (1) In Wuest's explanation of Son (Huios) in Hebrews chapter 1, we read: "The fact that the article is absent before the word "Son" emphasizes character, nature." "God spoke through One (Jesus) who is in the character of a Son." "He (Jesus) is the Logos, the total concept of Deity, throughout the Word of God, not in the sense of a spoken or a written word, but in the sense of a person who in Himself expresses all that God the Father is." (2)

When the word "son" refers to Jesus, it expresses Jesus' character or nature, not a physical Father/male offspring relationship. The word son (s) is also used metaphorically in the New Testament:

Sons Of the light Luke 16:8

Sons of the day 1 Thessalonians 5:5

Sons of peace, Luke 10:6

Sons of this world, Luke 16:8

Sons of disobedience Ephesians 2:2

Sons of the resurrection Luke 20:36

Sons of the bride-chamber Mark 2:19

It is essential to understand that the physical body of Jesus Christ was begotten at a point in time. God poured his fullness (nature and character) into Him: *"For it pleased the*

Father that in him should all fulness dwell..." (Colossians 1:19) again, *"For in him dwelleth all the fulness of the Godhead bodily."* (Colossians 2:9).

One final thought: Jesus is not the only one addressed as a "son of God." Those who believe in Jesus Christ are also called "sons of God" (1 John 3:2). We are not called "sons of God" because God physically fathered us. We are called "sons of God" because of our new, Christ-like nature and character. This fact supports my contention that the phrase "Son of God," referring to Jesus, does not describe a Father/Son relationship but rather His nature or character.

The Only Begotten

Another phrase describes Jesus Christ as "only begotten of the Father" (John 1:14) and "Only Son" (John 1:18, 3:16, 3:18, and 1 John 4:9). The Apostle John is the only writer who uses the Greek word "monogenes" (only begotten) in referring to Jesus Christ. While it is used of others in scripture about a parent/child relationship, most scholars recognize its unique application when used of Jesus Christ. W.E. Vine writes: "In John 3:16, the statement, 'God so loved that He gave His Only Son,' must not be taken to mean that Christ became the Only Begotten Son by incarnation. Incarnation means the state of being in bodily form and substance." [3] Vine points out something of importance. This phrase does not refer to the incarnation, the human birth of Jesus. It means something more, something different.

The meaning of this word becomes clear when God asks Abraham to sacrifice his son, Isaac, as an offering. God said to Abraham, *"Take your son, your only [Yachid] son Isaac, whom you love, and go to the land of Moriah, and offer him there as a burnt offering on one of the mountains of which I shall tell you"* (Gen. 22:2). The Apostle Paul also wrote about this event: *"By faith Abraham, when he was tried, offered up Isaac: and he that had received the promises offered up his only begotten (monogenes) son, Of whom it was said, That in Isaac shall thy seed be called:"* (Hebrews 11:17-18).

If we are to understand what "only begotten" means, it is essential to note that Isaac was not Abraham's only son. Abraham had two sons: Ishmael and Isaac. However, Isaac was the only son of promise, not Ishmael. Isaac was the son of the covenant. Although both were Abraham's sons, Isaac's relationship with Abraham was "unique," different from Ismael's. Knowing this gives us a better understanding of the word "monogenes": it means "a one-of-a-kind relationship." (see Yachid, page 19). It is not about the relationship that exists through procreation; it is about a unique, one-of-a-kind relationship. Jesus had a "one-of-a-kind" relationship with God; thus, He is the "only begotten" of the Father. There are many "sons of God" mentioned throughout the Bible. But only one is the "only begotten" of the Father: Jesus Christ.

Son of Man

"Son of man" is the counterpart to the phrase "Son of God." When both are understood, they reveal Jesus' dual nature as God/Man. Jesus often used the phrase "The Son of Man" in referring to Himself. In that Jesus did not have a human father, this phrase must be understood as referring to the character and nature of Jesus. Jesus referred to Himself in three ways: 1. His human condition (Matthew 11:19, Luke 7:34). 2. His imminent death and resurrection (Mark 8:31, 9:9, 14:21). 3. His second coming with all power to execute judgment (Matthew 24:27, Mark 8:38, Luke 17:24, see also Daniel 7:13-14).

Interestingly, the "Son of Man" never applies to Jesus Christ after his death, burial, and resurrection. During apostolic times, it was used only twice. Once, in the speech of Stephen (Acts 7:56), *"And said, Behold, I see the heavens opened, and the Son of man standing on the right hand of God."* Here, Stephen recalls Jesus' own words found in Matthew 26:64. A second time occurred during John's vision in Revelation 1:13, where he says he saw one "like unto the Son of Man," but, interestingly, John does not use the title directly.

The Holy Spirit

The Athanasian Creed states the Holy Spirit is one of three "persons" in the Godhead: "And the Catholic faith is this: that we worship one God in Trinity, and Trinity in Unity; neither confounding the Persons, nor dividing the

Essence, for there is one Person of the Father; another of the Son; and another of the Holy Ghost. But the Godhead of the Father, of the Son, and of the Holy Ghost, is all one; the Glory equal, the Majesty coeternal. Such as the Father is, such is the Son, and such is the Holy Ghost. The Father uncreated; the Son uncreated; and the Holy Ghost uncreated. The Father unlimited; the Son unlimited; and the Holy Ghost unlimited. The Father eternal; the Son eternal; and the Holy Ghost eternal. And yet they are not three eternals; but one eternal ...." The question is this: Is the Holy Spirit a person? (https://en.wikipedia.org/wiki/Athanasian_Creed)

The "personhood" of the Holy Spirit seems to be supported in the English translation of the New Testament, as the translators used masculine pronouns when translating the words "Spirit" and "Holy Spirit" as "he," "him," "his," and "himself." Their use of masculine pronouns appears to support the belief that the Holy Spirit is a person. But there is a problem. If the Holy Spirit were a person, the Holy Spirit would have to be gender-specific, i.e., male or female. This gender should be consistently reflected in Hebrew, Greek, and English translations of the scriptures. However, the gender of the Holy Spirit in the original languages is inconsistent in the scriptures. The inconsistency presented a problem for the translators.

Our English translation comes to us through Hebrew and Greek manuscripts. All three languages differ in how they treat the noun "Spirit." Both Hebrew and Greek assign gender to nouns. The Hebrew language assigns gender to nouns as either masculine or feminine. The Greek language assigns masculine, feminine, and neuter (neutral) genders. In the Greek language, the word "Spirit" (pneuma) is always rendered in the neuter (neutral), i.e., "pneuma (4151) is neuter, coming from (4154) (pneo); a current of air, i.e., breath (blast) or a breeze; by analogy or figurative a spirit, i.e. (human) the rational soul, (by implication) vital principle, mental disposition, etc., or (superhuman) an angel, dæmon, or (divine) God, Christ's spirit, the Holy Spirit:-ghost, life, spirit (-ual, -ually), mind. Compare (G5590) (psuche). (see also Breath, Breathe, Spirit and Wind)." (Strong's Greek and Hebrew Dictionary). Note: Strong's never translates "pneuma" as "person."

Unlike the Greek language, in the Hebrew language, "Spirit" (spirit) is ruach or ruah; it is feminine (Strong's 7307). In Aramaic, the word for Holy Spirit is also feminine. In the English version, the translators used masculine pronouns. So, the Spirit is neuter in Greek, feminine in Hebrew and Aramaic, and masculine in English translation. In the English translation, masculine pronouns describe the Holy Spirit (Ghost), comforter, and advocate. Despite the noun Spirit being neuter in the Greek New Testament when translated into English, the translators often used the noun with pronouns "he," "him," and "his" rather than the neuter "it," "its," "itself," "which" or "that." The translators, believing the Holy Spirit was a "person," had to ascribe a "gender," male or female, to the Spirit. They chose male. That is why they used masculine pronouns "he," "him," etc., when translating the "Holy Spirit."

The exception occurs with the words "comforter" and "advocate" in John's gospels. The words "comforter" and "advocate" describe the Holy Spirit. Both words are translations of another Greek word, "parakletos." Parakletos is a masculine noun. Some translators may have used the masculine noun parakletos to justify using masculine nouns when translating "Spirit" (Holy Spirit, Ghost) in the New Testament. If they did, were they correct in doing so? Let us see how John uses the word parakletos in his writings. The word "comforter" only appears four times in the New Testament, while the word "advocate" appears once; all five occurrences are in John's writings. Both words are translations of the same Greek word, parakletos. In John 14:15-17, we read of the "comforter" being sent; *"If ye love me, keep my commandments. And I will pray the Father, and he shall give you another Comforter (parakletos), that he may abide with you for ever; Even the Spirit of truth; whom the world cannot receive, because it seeth him not, neither knoweth him: but ye know him; for he dwelleth with you, and **shall be in you.**" (see also 14:26, 15:26 and 16:2).* Notice the use of the masculine pronouns "he" and "him" in referring to the Comforter. The question I would pose is this; why does the apostle John use the masculine pronouns in referring to the "comforter" in this and other passages?

The answer to the question, "Why does John use masculine pronouns when referring to the comforter"? is found in Verse 18: *"**I** will not leave you comfortless: **I will come to you.**"* Jesus said, "I will come to you...." In verse 20, we read, *"At that day ye shall know that I am in my Father, and ye in me, and **I in you.**"* Jesus is the "comforter" and "advocate," the "parakletos," according to the apostle John. This explains John's use of masculine pronouns in these passages, since Jesus was a man.

We find the same thing in 1 John 2:1: *"My little children, these things write I unto you, that ye sin not. And if any man sin, we have an advocate with the Father, Jesus Christ the righteous:"* In this passage, Jesus Christ is identified as the "advocate" or the "parakletos." As the advocate, it would have been proper to use the masculine noun parakletos and the masculine pronouns "he" and "him," since Jesus was masculine. While it would be proper to use the masculine in these passages, it would not be appropriate to use them when referring to the "Spirit" or "Holy Spirit" as the Greek word for "spirit" is neuter, not masculine. Sometimes we see the correct gender, neuter, used to refer to the Holy Spirit. In Romans 8:16, we read: *"The Spirit **itself** beareth witness with our spirit, that we are the children of God:"* (see also Matthew 10:20, Romans 8:26). Many scholars believe "neuter" is the correct gender when translating the word "Spirit" or "Ghost" in the New Testament.

Most scholars believe Jesus spoke Aramaic. Aramaic, not Hebrew, was the language used by Jews in Jesus' time. This is attested to as the New Testament has many examples of Jesus speaking Aramaic: Raca Matthew 5:22, Eli, Eli, lema sabachthani Matthew 27:46, Talitha cumi Mark 5:41, Ephphatha Mark 7:34, Abba Mark 14:36, Eli, Eli, lema sabachthani Mark 15:34, Rabboni John 20:16, Maranatha 1 Corinthians 16:22. When Jesus spoke the word

"Spirit," He would have used the Aramaic word "rucha" (ruach in Hebrew), not the Greek word "pneuma." This is important as both words, rucha (Aramaic) and ruach (Hebrew), are feminine in their respective language, not masculine. In John 14:15-17, we read: *"If ye love me, keep my commandments. And I will pray the Father, and he shall give you another **Comforter** (parakletos, masculine), that he may abide with you for ever; Even the **Spirit** (Greek, pneuma, neuter) of truth; whom the world cannot receive, because it seeth him not, neither knoweth him: but ye know him; for he dwelleth with you, and shall be in you."* In this passage, the word "Comforter" is in the masculine. However, the word "Spirit," as used by Jesus, would have been in the feminine in Aramaic. In this passage, the Comforter, the Holy Spirit, is referred to as both masculine and feminine. If the Holy Spirit were a person, this passage would be incomprehensible.

In Acts 5:1-10, we find an interesting story about a man named Ananias and his wife, Sapphira. They sold a "possession." They pledged the entire amount to God but kept part of it. Peter speaks to the husband Ananias, *"But Peter said, Ananias, why hath Satan filled thine heart to lie to the Holy Ghost and to keep back part of the price of the land?"* Peter told Ananias he lied to the Holy Spirit. According to the doctrine of the Trinity, the Holy Spirit (Ghost) is a separate, distinct person. As we read on, we see what Peter meant: *"Whiles it remained, was it not thine own? and after it was sold, was it not in thine own power? why hast thou conceived this thing in thine heart? thou hast* *not lied unto men, but **unto God**."* (Acts 5:3-4) Here, the Scriptures are clear, the Holy Spirit is identified as God, not as a separate "person."

Paul clears the matter up in a letter to the Thessalonians. He wrote: *"For God hath not called us unto uncleanness, but unto holiness. He therefore that despiseth, despiseth not man, but God, who hath also given unto us **his holy Spirit**."* (1 Thessalonians 4:8). Here, the Holy Spirit is identified as God's Spirit, not a "distinct" person. In the Hebrew account of creation, we read, *"And the **Spirit** (a feminine noun) of **God** (a masculine noun) moved upon the face of the waters."* (Genesis 1:2). In this verse, we have both masculine and feminine genders, referring to God. When Adam was created, we read, *"And God said, Let us make man in our image, after our likeness: and let them have dominion over the fish of the sea, and over the fowl of the air, and over the cattle, and over all the earth, and over every creeping thing that creepeth upon the earth." So God created man in his own image, in the image of God created he him; **male and female created he them**."* (Genesis 1:26-27). The "image and likeness" of God is, among other things, "male and female." We know this is correct as Eve, the woman, is taken out of Adam, the man.

God is depicted in scripture as possessing both maternal and paternal qualities. Because God possesses maternal and paternal qualities does not mean God is a "person," a man, or a woman. These speak to God's qualities and character, not gender.

To sum up: the word Spirit in Hebrew/Aramaic is feminine. In Greek, the word for Spirit is neuter, and in English translations, the Spirit is treated as masculine. As you can see, attempting to determine the "gender" of the Holy Spirit based on the noun's gender in scripture is problematic. The Holy Spirit is God's Spirit; therefore, God's Spirit may be masculine, feminine, or neutral, depending upon the context, not the gender. Jewish teachers understood this. One, Rabbi Kaplan, writes: "G-d has no body, no genitalia; therefore, the very idea that G-d is male, or female, is patently absurd. Although in the Talmudic part of the Torah and especially in Kabalah, G-d is referred to under the name 'Sh'chinah' - which is feminine, this is only to accentuate the fact that all the creation and nature are actually in the receiving end in reference to the creator and as no part of the creation can perceive the Creator outside of nature, it is adequate to refer to the divine presence in feminine form. We refer to G-d using masculine terms simply for convenience's sake because Hebrew has no neutral gender; G-d is no more male than a table is." (4) "The fact that we always refer to God as 'He' is also not meant to imply that the concept of sex or gender applies to God." (5)

There are many instances in the scriptures where the Holy Spirit is not a "person." The Holy Spirit is an oil (Psalms 45:7), God's breath (John 20:22), Wind (Acts 2:2), and Fire (Acts 2:3). The Holy Spirit is poured out (Acts 2:17-33), given as a gift (Acts 10:45), may be quenched (1 Thessalonians 5:19), baptizes believers (Matthew 3:11), likened to water (John 4:14), may be drunk (John 7:37-39).

Using the word "breath" to describe the Holy Spirit illustrates my point, as the Holy Spirit is neither male nor female. God's Spirit is acting in our world, immaterial, invisible, and powerful. Jesus said it in these words: *"The wind (pneuma) bloweth where it listeth, and thou hearest the sound thereof, but canst not tell whence it cometh, and whither it goeth: so is every one that is born of the Spirit."* (John 3:8).

Here are some truths to ponder. If the Holy Spirit were a "person," why is the Holy Spirit never worshipped in the Scriptures? Why didn't the apostle Paul address the Holy Spirit in his greetings to the churches? It would be untenable if the Holy Spirit were a person, coequal with the Father and Son. The scriptures record no one praying to the Holy Spirit (see Stephen's prayer Acts 7:55). Believers do not fellowship with the Holy Spirit (1 John 1:3); they have the fellowship "of" the Holy Spirit (2 Cor 13:14). The apostle tells us the Holy Spirit conceived Jesus: *"But while he thought on these things, behold, the angel of the Lord appeared unto him in a dream, saying, Joseph, thou son of David, fear not to take unto thee Mary thy wife: for that which is conceived in her is of the Holy Ghost."* (Matthew 1:20) Though the Holy Spirit conceived Jesus, Jesus never addresses the Holy Spirit as Father. Jewish scholars, teachers, and believers never understood the Holy Spirit to be a "person." That idea is foreign to them. Jewish prophets knew the Holy Spirit was not part of a Trinity. The Holy Spirit was and remained God's Spirit. The apostle Paul knew the Holy Spirit as the Spirit of "power, love, and a sound mind" (2 Timothy 1:7). When Mary was told she would conceive Jesus, the angel told her, "The **Holy Spirit** will come upon you ...", continuing, Luke wrote "**the power of the Highest**," which "will overshadow you." (Luke 1:35). Here, we read the Holy Spirit is the "power of the Highest," not a separate person.

The following observation is found in this curious statement by the apostle Paul *"That their hearts might be comforted, being knit together in love, and unto all riches of the full assurance of understanding, to the acknowledgment of the mystery of God, and of the Father, and of Christ:"* (Colossians 2:2). Paul wants the Colossians to know the *"mystery of God, and of the Father, and of Christ,"* but there is no mention of the Holy Spirit. Why? Paul, a Jew, a former Pharisee, understood, the Holy Spirit is God's Spirit. The Holy Spirit is not, could not be, a separate "person." Therefore, Paul was not "slighting" the Holy Spirit by his omission in this passage.

I will give the last word to The New Catholic Encyclopedia: "The majority of New Testament texts reveal God's spirit as something, not someone; this is especially seen in the parallelism between the spirit and the power of God. When a quasi-personal activity is ascribed to God's spirit, e.g., speaking, hindering, desiring, dwelling (Acts 8:29; Acts 16:7; Romans 8:9), one is not justified in concluding immediately that in these passages, God's spirit is regarded as a Person; the same expressions are also used in regard to rhetorically personified things or abstract ideas" In Acts, the use of the words 'Holy Spirit,' with or without an article, is rich and abundant. However, again, it is challenging to demonstrate personality from the texts." (6) In conclusion, the Scriptures do not support the Trinitarian belief of three persons in the Godhead.

Footnotes Chapter 8

1. W.E. Vine, Expository Dictionary of New Testament Words, Vol. 1, Set 7, Pg. 48

2. Wuest, Word Studies in the Greek New Testament, Vol. II, pg. 34

3. W.E. Vine, Expository Dictionary of New Testament Words, Vol. 3, page 140

4. Rabbi Aryeh Kaplan, Judaism 101

5. Rabbi Aryeh Kaplan, The Aryeh Kaplan Reader, Mesorah Publications (1983), p. 144

6. The New Catholic Encyclopedia, 2003, Vol. 13, "Spirit, Holy," p. 428

Chapter 9
Problems Examined

"And ye shall know the truth, and the truth shall make you free."
John 8:32

The following are problems the doctrine of the Trinity cannot resolve adequately. The Bible states that Jesus Christ is the Father: *"Jesus saith unto him, Have I been so long time with you, and yet hast thou not known me, Philip? he that hath seen me hath seen the Father; and how sayest thou then, Shew us the Father?"* (John 14:9). If one believes the Father is not the Son, and the Son is not the Father, how do we understand this?

The Bible also states the Holy Spirit is Jesus' Spirit: *"But ye are not in the flesh, but in the Spirit if so be that the Spirit of God dwell in you. Now if any man have not the Spirit of Christ, he is none of his."* (Romans 8:9) *"And because ye are sons, God hath sent forth the Spirit of his Son into your hearts, crying, Abba, Father."* (Galatians 4:6). We are, again, confronted with the question I asked earlier; "how do we understand this?" The question "how do we understand this?" repeatedly arises when we compare scriptures. As examples, I submit the following questions.

Who raised Jesus from the dead?

The Father

"Therefore, we are buried with him by baptism into death: that like as Christ was raised up from the dead by the glory of the Father, even so we also should walk in newness of life." (Romans 6:4).

In this passage the Father raises Jesus from the dead.

The Son

"Jesus answered and said unto them, destroy this temple, and in three days I will raise it up." (John 2:19).

In this passage Jesus claims to raise Himself from the grave.

The Holy Spirit

"But if the Spirit of him that raised up Jesus from the dead dwell in you, he that raised up Christ from the dead shall also quicken your mortal bodies by his Spirit that dwelleth in you." (Romans 8:11).

In this passage it is the Spirit that raised Jesus from the dead. We find that the same thing happens with the following examples.

Who placed the ministries?

God

"And God hath set some in the church, first apostles, secondarily prophets, thirdly teachers, after that miracles, then gifts of healings, helps, governments, diversities of tongues." (1 Corinthians 12:28).

The Son

"But unto every one of us is given grace according to the measure of the gift of Christ. Wherefore he saith, When he ascended up on high, he led captivity captive, and gave gifts unto men. (Now that he ascended, what is it but that he also descended first into the lower parts of the earth? He that descended is the same also that ascended up far above all heavens, that he might fill all things. And he gave some, apostles; and some, prophets; and some, evangelists; and some, pastors and teachers;" (Ephesians 4:6-11).

The Holy Spirit:

"Take heed therefore unto yourselves, and to all the flock, over the which the Holy Ghost hath made you overseers, to feed the church of God, which he hath purchased with his own blood." (Acts 20:28).

Who indwells the believer today?

God

"Know ye that ye are the temple of God and that the Spirit of God dwelleth in you?" (1 Corinthians 3:16).

The Son

"At that day ye shall know that I am in my Father, and ye in me, and I in you." (John 14:20).

The Holy Spirit

"What? know ye not that your body is the temple of the Holy Ghost which is in you, which ye have of God, and ye are not your own?" (I Corinthians 6:19).

Who answers prayer?

The Father

"Ye have not chosen me, but I have chosen you, and ordained that you should go and bring forth fruit., and that your fruit should remain: that whatsoever ye shall ask of the Father in my name, he may give it to you." (John 15:16).

The Son

"And whatsoever ye shall ask in my name, that will I do, that the Father may be glorified in the Son." (John 14:13).

On whom shall we believe?

God

"Verily, verily, I say unto you, He that heareth my word, and believeth on him that sent me, hath everlasting life, and shall not come into condemnation: but is passed from death unto life." (John 5:24).

The Son

"For God so loved the world, that he gave his only begotten Son, that whosoever believeth in him should not perish, but have everlasting life." (John 3:16).

The Prayers of Jesus Christ

One area of confusion regarding the Godhead and the deity of Jesus Christ occurs when Jesus prays to the Father. Some believe Jesus' praying to the Father proves He is separate from the Father. If Jesus is separate, that would suggest "subordinationism," as Origen and others taught. The Scriptures clear up the confusion and show Jesus is not subordinate.

In the New Testament, several words are translated "to ask" or "to pray." We will look at two Greek words translated as "ask" or "pray." The first is "aiteō," which means "to ask from" or pray to "a higher authority." It is the word used when believers ask or pray to God (Ephesians 3:20). But there is an entirely different word used whenever Jesus asked or prayed. That word is "erotao," which means "to ask from" or "pray to" an equal authority. This same word is used in scripture, where believers ask each other anything, because they would obviously be asking among equals.

The following quote from W.E. Vine sheds significant light on this: "AITEO," "to ask," is to be distinguished from No. 2 EROTAO."

1. AITEO more frequently suggests the attitude of a suppliant, the petition of one who is lesser in position than he to whom the petition is made; e.g., in the case of men in asking something from God, Mat 7:7; a child from a parent, Mat 7:9, 10; a subject from a king, Act 12:20; priests and people from Pilate, Luke 23:23 (RV, "asking" for AV, "requiring"); a beggar from a passerby, Act 3:2. With reference to petitioning God, this verb is found in Paul's epistles in Eph 3:20; Col 1:9; in James four times, James 1:5, 6; 4:2, 3; in 1 John, five times, 1Jo 3:22; 5:14, 15 (twice), 16. See BEG, CALL FOR, A, No. 7, CRAVE, DESIRE, REQUIRE."

2. EROTAO more frequently suggests that the petitioner is on a footing of equality or familiarity with the person he requests. A king uses it in making a request of another king (Luke 14:32); of the Pharisee who "desired" Christ that He would eat with him (Luke 7:36), an indication of the inferior conception he had of Christ; Luke 7:36; cp. Luke 11:37; John 9:15; 18:19.

In this respect, it is significant that Jesus never used "aiteo" in making a request to the Father. W.E. Vine writes:

"The consciousness of His equal dignity, of His potent and prevailing intercession, speaks out in this, that as often as He asks, or declares that He will ask anything of the Father, it is always erotao, an asking, upon equal terms, John 14:16; 16:26; 17:9,15,20, never aiteo, that He uses. Martha, on the contrary, plainly reveals her poor, unworthy conception of His person, that ... she ascribes that aiteo to Him which He never ascribes to Himself, John 11:22 ". (1)

Following the death of Lazarus, his sister Martha asked Jesus to ask God to raise her dead brother. Martha's error was that she asked Jesus to ask (aiteo) to a higher authority recognizing Jesus as a man, *"But I know, that even now, whatsoever thou wilt ask (aiteo) of God, God will give it thee."* (John 11:22). Instead of praying to God Jesus declared He would raise Lazarus; *"Jesus said unto her, I am the resurrection, and the life: he that believeth in me, though he were dead, yet shall he live:"* Martha realizes that He is the Christ; *"Believest thou this? She saith unto him, Yea, Lord: I believe that thou art the Christ, the Son of God, which should come into the world."* (John 11:22-27). Remember, the key to understanding the mystery of godliness is the dual nature of Jesus Christ. He was, is, truly God and truly a man in one. In all of history, He is the only one.

So, how are we to understand Jesus praying to God? There were many areas in which Jesus, as a man, humbled Himself and became a "servant." It was especially true in areas where the scriptures declare a man should humble himself. Remember, He was the God-man, and the scriptures command all flesh (man) to come to God in prayer. *"O thou that hearest prayer, unto thee shall all flesh come."* (Psalms 65:2). Jesus Christ, as a man, had to fulfill the Word of God at every point to satisfy divine justice, and He did, even in humbling Himself, to pray as a man and dying on the cross.

Another question that frequently comes up with new Christians is: "In what name do we pray"? The scriptures answer this question through the words of Jesus Christ. In John's gospel, Jesus said, *"If ye shall ask any thing in **my name**, I will do it."* (14:14). In the 16th chapter of John, we read: *"And in that day ye shall ask me nothing. Verily, verily, I say unto you, Whatsoever ye shall ask the Father in **my name**, he will give it you."* (John 16:23). We are to pray in Jesus' Name.

There are examples in the New Testament where someone prays to Jesus. In the 7th chapter of Acts, we read about a deacon named Stephen who was brought before the Sanhedrin for preaching the gospel. Here is the account of his testimony: *"When they heard these things, they were cut to the heart, and they gnashed on him with their teeth. But he, being full of the Holy Ghost, looked up stedfastly into heaven, and saw the glory of God, and Jesus standing on the right hand of God, And said, Behold, I see the heavens opened, and the Son of man standing on the right hand of God. Then they cried out with a loud voice, and stopped their ears, and ran upon him with one accord, And cast him out of the city, and stoned him: and the witnesses laid down their clothes at a young man's feet, whose name was Saul. And they stoned Stephen,* **calling upon God, and saying, Lord Jesus, receive my spirit**. *And he kneeled down, and cried with a loud voice, Lord, lay not this sin to their charge. And when he had said this, he fell asleep."* (Acts 7:54-60) If there is any doubt as to the Name we are to use in praying, the following passage puts the question beyond dispute: *"And whatsoever ye do in word or deed, do all in the name of the Lord Jesus, giving thanks to God and the Father by him."* (Colossians 3:17).

The Right Hand of God

"Who is gone into heaven, and is on the right hand of God; angels and authorities and powers being made subject unto him." 1 Peter 3:22

If Jesus is God, why does the Bible say He is on the "right hand of God"? Admittedly, some scripture passages appear to suggest separateness or distinctiveness in the Godhead. The passage above, 1 Peter 3:22, is one. How are we to understand what Peter meant in writing that Jesus "is on the right hand of God"?

To understand the statement, we need to understand the use of metaphors in the Bible. A metaphor is a comparison of two things. It uses figurative language to represent something. The purpose of the metaphor is to make a difficult concept or idea more familiar or understandable to the reader. Some biblical examples are: *"The law of the wise is a fountain of life, to depart from the snares of death."* (Proverbs 13:14). The "fountain of life" suggests a continuing source of instruction and wisdom. In Isaiah 64:8, the prophet writes, *"... we are the clay; you are the potter."*

God, the potter, is the one who controls or creates, not the clay. A famous metaphor comes to mind from the 23rd Psalms. Here we read, *"the Lord is my shepherd ...."* The shepherd takes care of the flock, protecting and providing for it, as does God. In Revelation, we find three wonderful metaphors; *"Let us be glad and rejoice and give honour to him: for the marriage of the Lamb is come, and his wife hath made herself ready."* (Revelation 19:7). There are three metaphors in this passage: The Lamb (Jesus), the "bride" (the church) and the "marriage," which represents the complete union of both.

Let us return to the passage under consideration, *"Who is gone into heaven, and is **on the right hand of God**; angels and authorities and powers being made subject unto him."* (1 Peter 3:22, emphasis mine). The words "right hand" in this passage are used metaphorically. So, what does "sitting on the right hand of God" mean? Young's Literal Translation helps us understand this passage as (Christ): *"who is at the right hand of God, having gone on to heaven--messengers, and authorities, and powers, having been subjected to him."* (1 Peter 3:22). He renders it as "at the right hand" not "on the right hand ..." It speaks to the power and authority that Jesus possesses. The latter portion of 1 Peter 3:22 supports this: *"angels and authorities and powers being made subject unto him."* (see also the Bible in Basic English).

This same metaphor is used in Paul's letter to the Ephesians: *"Which he wrought in Christ, when he raised him from the dead, and set him **at his own right hand** in the heavenly places, Far above all principality, and power, and might, and dominion, and every name that is named, not only in this world, but also in that which is to come: And hath put all things under his feet, and gave him to be the head over all things to the church, Which is his body, the fulness of him that filleth all in all."* (Ephesians 1:20-23). Here we read Jesus is "at" the right hand not "on" it. Let us continue reading the next chapter: *"And you hath he quickened, who were dead in trespasses and sins; ... But God, who is rich in mercy, for his great love wherewith he loved us, Even when we were dead in sins, hath quickened us together with Christ, (by grace ye are saved;) And hath **raised us up together, and made us sit together in heavenly places in Christ Jesus:"*** (Ephesians 2:1-6 emphasis mine) Note in chapter 2, verse 1: "you," the believer has been "raised up" together (with Jesus Christ) to sit together in heavenly places. We can all agree that this passage is not to be understood literally. It refers, metaphorically, to believers having power and authority today through Jesus Christ.

There is a great deal hidden from the casual reader in these passages. To begin with, in scripture, we find that the "right hand" is important. It is used to bestow the blessing upon the eldest son while the younger son receives his blessing from his father's left hand. This is significant when we understand that the elder son's inheritance was twice as much as the younger son's. We read in Genesis 48:13-19 that when Joseph's father, Israel, blessed his two sons, he purposely switched hands because he wanted the younger to receive the greater blessing or portion. *"And Joseph took them both, Ephraim in his right hand toward Israel's left hand, and Manasseh in his left hand toward Israel's right hand, and brought them near unto him. And Israel stretched out his right hand, and laid it upon Ephraim's head, who was the younger, and his left hand upon Manasseh's head, guiding his hands wittingly; for Manasseh was the firstborn. And he blessed Joseph, and said, God, before whom my fathers Abraham and Isaac did walk, the God which fed me all my life long unto this day, The Angel which redeemed me from all evil, bless the lads; and let my name be named on them, and the name of my fathers Abraham and Isaac; and let them grow into a multitude in the midst of the earth. And when Joseph saw that his father laid his right hand upon the head of Ephraim, it displeased him: and he held up his father's hand, to remove it from Ephraim's head unto Manasseh's head. And Joseph said unto his father, Not so, my father: for this is the firstborn; put thy right hand upon his head. And his father refused, and said, I know it, my son, I know it: he also shall become a people, and he also shall be great: but truly his younger brother shall be greater than he, and his seed shall become a multitude of nations."* In this passage, the "right hand" is a metaphor for the extra blessing the firstborn was supposed to receive.

It appears the "double portion," going to the firstborn, began in the time of Moses: *"If a man has two wives, one greatly loved, and the other hated, and the two of them have had children by him; and if the first son is the child of the hated wife: then when he gives his property to his sons for their heritage, he is not to put the son of his loved one in the place of the first son, the son of the hated wife: But he is to give his first son his birthright, and twice as great a part of his property: for he is the first-fruits of his strength and the right of the first son is his."* (Deuteronomy 21:15-17 BBE).

Interestingly, none of the prominent "firstborn" sons received the double portion mentioned in Deuteronomy. Cain was the firstborn, but Abel was chosen. After Cain murdered Abel, Adam and Eve had another son, Seth. Seth received the blessing. Isaac received the double portion, though Ishmael was firstborn. Esau was first born. Jacob was secondborn. Jacob received the blessing, not Esau. The youngest, not the oldest, received the extra blessings. This is also true about the Church. Israel was the "firstborn," while the Church was the "secondborn." Though Israel was first, the Church is the one that received the double portion, i.e., grace and the indwelling of the Holy Spirit. Scripture tells us that Jesus is called the "second man, Adam." Through the first man, "Adam," we received physical life and death; through the second "man Adam," Jesus, we receive eternal life, the double blessing! (I Cor. 15:45-48).

The prophet Isaiah also used a metaphor in referring to the Messiah: *"Who hath believed our report? and to whom is the **arm of the LORD** revealed?"* Who is the "arm of the LORD"? Isaiah tells us who he is by using metaphors: *"For he shall grow up before him as a tender plant, and as* *a root out of a dry ground: he hath no form nor comeliness; and when we shall see him, there is no beauty that we should desire him. He is despised and rejected of men; a man of sorrows, and acquainted with grief: and we hid as it were our faces from him; he was despised, and we esteemed him not....*" (Isaiah 53:1-3). Who is the subject of this passage? It is unmistakable that the prophet Isaiah is writing about the Messiah, Jesus Christ. He identifies the Messiah as the "arm of the LORD." Is Jesus sitting on God's hand, standing on it, or is He the arm of the Lord? This apparent conflict is quickly resolved when we realize the "right hand of God" and "the arm of the Lord" are to be understood as metaphors, not literally.

The use of metaphors becomes apparent when we compare the following two scriptures: *"Jesus saith unto him, Thou hast said: nevertheless I say unto you, Hereafter shall ye see the **Son of man sitting** on the right hand of power, and coming in the clouds of heaven."* (Matthew 26:64). In the following passage, we see something slightly different: *"And said, Behold, I see the heavens opened, and the Son of man **standing** on the right hand of God."* (Acts 7:56). In the final judgment, the right hand symbolizes acceptance into God's Kingdom, and the left-hand eternal rejection *"And he the sheep on his right hand, but the goats on the left."* (Matthew 25:33).

Using metaphors, we learn that Jesus holds the position of power and authority. The position of acceptance, strength, and honor. These all belong to Him. Matthew 28:18 reads: *"And Jesus came and spake unto them, saying,*

All power is given unto me in heaven and in earth." This passage puts the question beyond dispute. Jesus is not sitting on God's hand; the metaphor means Jesus has "all power … in heaven and earth".

Footnotes Chapter 9

1. W.E. Vines An Expository Dictionary of New Testament Words, pg. 79

Chapter 10
A Contradiction Resolved

"Go, therefore, and teach all nations, baptizing them in the name of the Father, and of the Son, and of the Holy Ghost." (Matthew 28:19).

  The passage above is a quote from Jesus to His disciples. It seems to support the Trinitarian position of three persons in the Godhead, as the "Father, Son, and Holy Ghost" are mentioned. This passage is also used to support baptisms using the "triune" formula, i.e., "Father, Son, and Holy Ghost." I would ask, "How did the apostles understand this command?" If we can discover the names the apostles and disciples used when baptizing new believers, that would answer the question. We find the answer to this question just a few days after Jesus gave the commandment in Matthew 28:19. It occurred on the day of Pentecost. On that day, the outpouring of the Holy Spirit and the birth of the Church occurred. And something else happened; the apostles performed the first baptisms.

  First, a little background: the Romans ruled the known world at the time of Christ. According to the scriptures, there were three "classes" of people: Jews, Samaritans, and Gentiles. The Jews were the dominant group in and around Jerusalem. The Samaritans claimed to be descendants of the Northern tribes of Ephraim and Manasseh. The Jews believed the Samaritans were not Jews at all. In 721 B.C., the Assyrians captured the Northern

Kingdom. Many Jews fled, but some stayed behind, and among the Jews who stayed behind, some married Assyrians. This "group" that intermarried became known as Samaritans.

For this reason, the Samaritans, who were half Jew and half Gentile, were looked down upon by the Jews. The third "group" was Gentile. These three "groups" would have comprised "all the nations" to the first disciples. So, what happened on Pentecost, a few days after Jesus commanded them to baptize new believers? As I mentioned earlier, the disciples were instructed, by Jesus, to baptize in the "name of the Father, Son, and Holy Spirit". However, we know that is not what they did! What happened is recorded in the book of Acts: *"Then Peter said unto them, Repent, and be baptized every one of you in the name of Jesus Christ for the remission of sins, and ye shall receive the gift of the Holy Ghost."* (Acts 2:38). Peter, who was present when Jesus gave the command in Matthew 28:19, baptized the new believers in "the name of Jesus Christ" not the name of the "Father, Son, and Holy Ghost."

Luke's account tells the reader that Peter was *"filled with the Holy Ghost"* (Acts 2:4) when he instructed the new converts to be baptized in the name of Jesus Christ. Did Peter misspeak? Was he disobeying Jesus' command in Matthew 28:19 to baptize in the "name of the Father, Son, and Holy Spirit"? No. Peter was "filled with the Holy Ghost." How could he have misspoken? Jesus told Peter, and the others, that after the Holy Spirit had come to them, the Spirit *"would guide them into all truth."* (John 16:13).

On the day of Pentecost, the Holy Spirit had come. And we know Peter was speaking under the power of the Holy Spirit when he told the people to be baptized in the name of Jesus Christ. Now, the question is, which baptism is the correct one? Is it in the name of the "Father, Son, and Holy Ghost" or the name of "Jesus Christ"? The following scriptures reveal the answer.

The next baptism takes place in Samaria. The Samaritans were the second group, following the Jews on Pentecost, to receive baptism. Phillip went down to Samaria and preached Christ to the Samaritans. When they believed him, they were baptized. Luke recorded it here: *"But when they believed Philip preaching the things concerning the kingdom of God, and the name of Jesus Christ, they were baptized, both men and women. Then Simon himself believed also: and when he was baptized, he continued with Philip, and wondered, beholding the miracles and signs which were done."* (Acts 8:12-13). Notice that Luke does not record the name or formula in baptizing these new converts. But the reader quickly discovers how they were baptized, as Luke mentions in the following verses. *"Now when the apostles which were at Jerusalem heard that Samaria had received the word of God, they sent unto them Peter and John: Who, when they were come down, prayed for them, that they might receive the Holy Ghost: (For as yet he was fallen upon none of them: only **they were baptized in the name of the Lord Jesus**."* (Acts 8:14-16 emphasis mine). Again, we read the Samaritan converts were not baptized using the formula in

Matthew 28:19; they were baptized in the name of Jesus Christ.

The Jews were the first to come into the body of Christ on Pentecost (Acts 2:38). Then, the Samaritans were brought in by the preaching of Phillip (Acts 8). That left the third group, the Gentiles. Enter Peter and the critical vision he experienced. The account begins in Acts 10:1. Here, we read of a man named Cornelius. He was a Gentile. He was also a "devout man, and one that feared God with all his house." (Acts 10:2). God spoke to Cornelius and told him about Peter. He told Cornelius to send for Peter. On the next day, Peter was *"upon the housetop to pray about the sixth hour."* (Acts 10:9). While praying, God gave Peter a vision, a unique vision.

In the vision, Peter sees a sheet let down from heaven; upon it are unclean animals. Peter, being a Jew, would not eat these unclean animals. Here is the account: *"On the morrow, as they went on their journey, and drew nigh unto the city, Peter went up upon the housetop to pray about the sixth hour: And he became very hungry, and would have eaten: but while they made ready, he fell into a trance, And saw heaven opened, and a certain vessel descending unto him, as it had been a great sheet knit at the four corners, and let down to the earth: Wherein were all manner of four-footed beasts of the earth, and wild beasts, and creeping things, and fowls of the air. And there came a voice to him, Rise, Peter; kill, and eat. But Peter said, Not so, Lord; for I have never eaten anything that is common or unclean. And the voice spake unto him again the second time, What God hath cleansed, that call not thou common. This was done thrice: and the vessel was received up again into heaven. Now while Peter doubted in himself what this vision which he had seen should mean, behold, the men which were sent from Cornelius had made enquiry for Simon's house, and stood before the gate, and called, and asked whether Simon, which was surnamed Peter, were lodged there."* (Acts 10:9-18).

Peter, realizing God was using unclean animals as a type of Gentile, accompanies the men to the house of Cornelius. While there, he preached Christ unto them. What happens next is remarkable. *"While Peter yet spake these words, the Holy Ghost fell on all them which heard the word. And they of the circumcision which believed were astonished, as many as came with Peter, because that on the Gentiles also was poured out the gift of the Holy Ghost. For they heard them speak with tongues and magnify God. Then answered Peter, Can any man forbid water, that these should not be baptized, which have received the Holy Ghost as well as we? And he **commanded them to be baptized in the name of the Lord.** Then prayed they him to tarry certain days."* (Acts 10:44-48). Notice, again, Peter uses the "name of the Lord," i.e., Jesus, not the formula found in Matthew 28:19. With the inclusion of the Gentiles into the church, they had laid the foundation. The Jews, Samaritans, and Gentiles had heard the Gospel. But our quest does not end here. There remained other baptisms that Luke recorded. One of them was the baptism of Saul, whom we know as Paul. Saul "made havoc" on the early church. He was a

Pharisee and very zealous for the law. He saw the church, the followers of Christ, as a sect that must be dealt with harshly. On his way to Damascus, Syria, he suddenly sees a bright light from the heavens. Falling, Saul hears a voice speak to him *"And he fell to the earth and heard a voice saying unto him, Saul, Saul, why persecutest thou me? And he said, Who art thou, Lord? And the Lord said, I am Jesus whom thou persecutest: it is hard for thee to kick against the pricks. And he trembling and astonished said, Lord, what wilt thou have me to do? And the Lord said unto him, Arise, and go into the city, and it shall be told thee what thou must do. And the men which journeyed with him stood speechless, hearing a voice, but seeing no man. And Saul arose from the earth; and when his eyes were opened, he saw no man: but they led him by the hand and brought him into Damascus. And he was three days without sight, and neither did eat nor drink."* (Acts 9:4-9).

When Saul arrives in Damascus, he is met by a man God sent to him, Ananias. At first, Ananias feared Saul; he did not want to go. But he was persuaded by God. Here is Luke's account of what follows: *"And Ananias went his way and entered into the house; and putting his hands on him said, Brother Saul, the Lord, even Jesus, that appeared unto thee in the way as thou camest, hath sent me, that thou mightest receive thy sight, and be filled with the Holy Ghost. And immediately there fell from his eyes as it had been scales: and he received sight forthwith, and arose, and was baptized "* (Acts 9:17-18). Of interest to us is this, Luke does not record "how" Saul was baptized. Did Ananias use the name of Jesus or the formula found in Matthew 28:19 when he baptized Saul? However, we can deduce that Ananias used the name of Jesus when he baptized Saul, since Saul (Paul) used the same name when he baptized others.

Here is what happened following his baptism, Saul, now referred to as Paul, immediately began to preach the Gospel. In Acts 19, we find Paul in Ephesus. Something telling occurs during his visit at Ephesus. *"And it came to pass, that, while Apollos was at Corinth, Paul having passed through the upper coasts came to Ephesus: and finding certain disciples, He said unto them, have ye received the Holy Ghost since ye believed? And they said unto him, we have not so much as heard whether there be any Holy Ghost. And he said unto them, unto what then were ye baptized? And they said, Unto John's baptism. Then said Paul, John verily baptized with the baptism of repentance, saying unto the people, that they should believe on him which should come after him, that is, on Christ Jesus. When they heard this, they were baptized in the name of the Lord Jesus."* (Acts 19:1-5). I find it interesting that Paul, realizing they had not received the Holy Spirit, asked them about their water baptism experience. Paul asks, "... unto what then were you baptized?" They answered, "John's baptism." Paul tells them they need to be re-baptized. He then baptizes them in "the name of the Lord Jesus." Now the question. Why would Paul baptize them in the name of Jesus instead of the formula found in Matthew? Answer: Ananias, apparently, baptized Paul in the name of Jesus as Paul is baptizing the men and women in the name of Jesus Christ.

Paul was drawing upon his personal experience when he instructed them in baptism.

This completes the record of baptisms that took place on and after Pentecost, the giving of the Holy Spirit, and the creation of the church. The Jew, Samaritan, and Gentiles had all heard the gospel, were filled with the Holy Spirit, and were baptized in the name of the Lord Jesus Christ. In the entire Bible, we cannot find one instance in which the formula found in Matthew 28:19, "Father, Son, and Holy Spirit," was used when baptizing new believers. Not one. Despite the overwhelming biblical evidence that all baptisms were in Jesus' Name, many churches use the titles found in Matthew 28:19.

Some question the authenticity of the Matthew 28:19 passage. Was it included in Matthew's original writings, or did a copyist add it later? This is the subject of much debate, with both sides offering persuasive arguments. It is my opinion it does not matter though I suspect it was added. A simple reading of the passage holds the answer to harmonizing the formula "Father, Son, and Holy Spirit" with the "name of Jesus Christ."

Let us reread Matthew 28:19, *"Go ye therefore, and teach all nations, baptizing them in the name of the Father, and of the Son and of the Holy Ghost."* The first thing to note is this; Jesus said, "baptizing them in "the name," not "the names" of the "Father, Son, and Holy Spirit." In the Greek text, the word "name" is in the "singular," not the "plural." It is significant because this suggests there is one name for the Father, Son, and Holy Spirit. Secondly, the "Father," "Son," and "Holy Spirit" are not proper names; they are titles. As an example, I am a "father" and a "son," but my name is Harold. The words "father" and "son" describe attributes, characteristics of me, but it is not my name. To my children, I am known as their father. To my parents, I am known as their son. But I am only one person. The same is true of God. The word Father describes an attribute or characteristic of God, not His name. In the Old Testament, his name was "I AM" or "YHWH." In the New Testament, we know there is only one name, not three, given to us, the Name of Jesus. *"Neither is there salvation in any other: for there is none other name under heaven given among men, whereby we must be saved."* (Acts 4:12).

What is the name of the Father? What is the name of the Holy Spirit? The Lord Jesus Christ reveals the name of the Father and the Holy Spirit. In John 5:43, we discover the name of the Father: *"I am come in my Father's name, and ye receive me not: if another shall come in his own name, him ye will receive."* Jesus also reveals the "name" the Holy Spirit bears: *"But the Comforter, which is the Holy Ghost, whom the Father will send in my name, he shall teach you all things, and bring all things to your remembrance, whatsoever I have said unto you."* (John 14:26). This passage explains why the Apostle's, despite having received the triune "formula" in Matthew 28:19, baptized believers in the name of the Lord Jesus Christ.

The New Testament is clear; there is only "one name" given by which we "must be saved": Jesus Christ.

Although a contradiction seems to exist between Matthew 28:19 and Acts 2:38, none exists. The name of the Father, the name of the Son, and the name of the Holy Spirit is Jesus Christ. That the church baptizes using the triune formula instead of the name of Jesus Christ should testify to the enormous influence a man's doctrine or creed can have, e.g., the Trinity. Though all baptisms, on and after Pentecost, were in the name of Jesus Christ (or the Lord Jesus Christ, etc.), most churches today continue to use and insist upon the incorrect, triune baptism. The Scriptures teach us they are mistaken.

Chapter 11
God's Glory Hidden in a Tent

"By a new and living way, which he hath consecrated for us, through the veil, that is to say, his flesh;"
Hebrews 10:20

The Bible records several theophanies of God. A theophany is a visible manifestation of the invisible God. In one theophany, God appeared as an angel unto Abraham. *"And the LORD appeared unto him in the plains of Mamre: and he sat in the tent door in the heat of the day..."* (Genesis 18:1). In another, Moses saw God in a burning bush (Exodus 3:3-6). Isaiah, Amos, Jeremiah, Ezekiel, and Zechariah saw God in visions and dreams. In the book of Job, Eliphaz tells us of his encounter with God: *"In thoughts from the visions of the night, when deep sleep falleth on men, Fear came upon me, and trembling, which made all my bones to shake. Then a spirit passed before my face; the hair of my flesh stood up:"* (Job 4:14-15). The most significant theophany of God, however, was through the birth of Jesus. It was at this moment in time that the invisible God took on a human body. The apostle John describes this birth with these words, *"And the Word made flesh and dwelt among us..."* (John 1:14). This theophany of God is foreshadowed in the Tabernacle in the wilderness.

The Tabernacle was a "tent" that served as a temporary Temple during the Exodus of the Jews from Egypt. God designed it to meet the needs of a nomadic people, i.e., it was movable. The Tabernacle would serve as the meeting place between God and Israel as Israel wandered in the desert for forty years. It was here, in the Tabernacle, that God would meet with the High Priest as he offered up prayers and gave offerings on behalf of the people: *"And there will I meet with thee and I will commune with thee from above the mercy seat, front between the two cherubim which are upon the Ark of the Testimony."* (Exodus 25:22). What is important to us is this; this "tent," the Tabernacle, held a secret. We must look at the Tabernacle in the wilderness to discover the secret. We begin our search in the book of Exodus, about the time of Israel's escape from Egypt. As Israel walked through the desert, God "walked" with them: *"Then a cloud covered the tent of the congregation, and the glory of the Lord filled the Tabernacle."* (Exodus 40:34).

Here we learn that God's plan was always to be with His people, to dwell among them. They always placed His tent, the Tabernacle, in the center of the Tribes of Israel. The Tabernacle was the focal point of the Israelites as they wandered for forty years. The Lion Handbook to the Bible, referring to Exodus 40:34, reads, "The Lord in His glory had actually come to dwell amongst His people. This is the supreme significance of the Tabernacle." (page 176). To dwell with his people has always been a desire of God. The illustration below depicts the Tabernacle in the Wilderness. Moses constructed it, following the specific instructions given to him by God. (Exodus 25:9). The apostle John knew the Tabernacle was a type of Jesus Christ and His Gospel. This was the "secret."

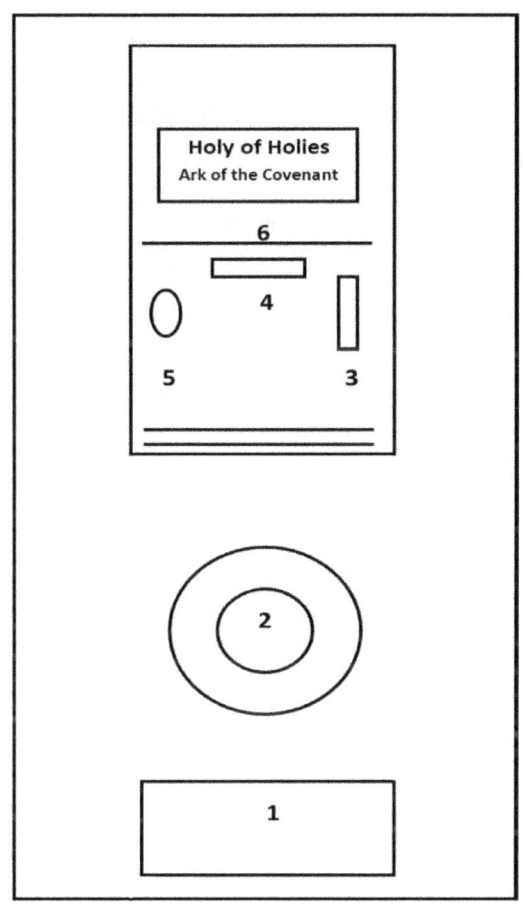

1. Altar of Sacrifice   2. Laver of Brass
3. Table /Shewbread   4. Altar of Incense
5. Lampstand   6. 2nd Veil

    As we enter, we first encounter the Altar of Sacrifice (1). Here the Priest would offer burnt offerings, a type of the sacrifice of Jesus Christ. The next item is the Laver of Brass (2). The Priest had to wash before he entered the Holy Place. The penalty was death if he did not wash. (Exodus 30:18-20). In the Messianic age, the Laver of Brass was a type of baptism, a washing. And as washing was required of the Jewish Priest, baptism is a requirement for believers today. (Acts 2:38).

Next, we encounter the first veil as we prepare to enter the Holy Place. Once inside the Holy Place, we see the Table of Shewbread (3), an Altar of Incense (4), and a Lampstand (5). The Shewbread is a type of Christ, "The bread of Life." (John 6:35). The Altar of Incense represents prayer, and the Lampstand represents the "light of the world" (John 8:12). Interestingly, this Lampstand was the only light source inside the Holy Place. There were no windows. Finally, we confront the second veil (6). Beyond this second veil is the Holy of Holies. Here we find the Ark of the Covenant, also known as the Ark of Testimony. God's glory would appear between two cherubim sitting on the Mercy Seat.

The contents of the Ark of the Covenant are telling. There are two Tablets upon which the Ten Commandments were written, Aaron's rod that budded and a bowl of Manna. Each item spoke of God's love, leadership, and provision for the people. The Ten Commandments would remind them of the covenant God entered with them. The rod of Aaron represented the leadership God chose for them, Moses and Aaron. The bowl of Manna would remind them of God's provision for them as they wandered in the desert. These items would also remind them of their rebellion and rejection of God's provisions. They broke the ten commandments, rejected God's leadership, i.e., Moses and Aaron, and complained about the Manna that God fed them. All these items would serve as a continual reminder of God's faithfulness despite their rebelliousness.

However, there was something more. It often goes unnoticed, the Mercy Seat. The Mercy Seat was a golden lid. On top of the Mercy Seat were two cherubim—one cherub at each end. There was a space between them for the Glory of God to rest. The Mercy Seat was placed over the items in the Ark. Despite the sinful rebellion against God's leadership and a rejection of His commandments and provisions, the "mercy" seat would cover them all. The mercy seat speaks to Christ's great gift of mercy.

The Tabernacle holds one more type: a key to understanding the deity of Jesus Christ. It is found in the second veil. This veil was a thick, long, high curtain about 10' x 10'. It stood before the priest and the people, preventing them from seeing or going into the Holy of Holies. Why? Because the presence of God dwelled there, behind the veil, above the mercy seat. The only person allowed to enter the Holy of Holies was the High Priest, on specific days, to minister on behalf of the people. If a person were to see God's glory, it would mean his or her death. *"Therefore thou and thy sons with thee shall keep your priest's office for every thing of the altar, and within the vail; and ye shall serve: I have given your priest's office unto you as a service of gift:*

and the stranger that cometh nigh shall be put to death." (Numbers 18:7).

The primary purpose of the veil was to hide God's glory and presence from the people. This insight regarding the veil is a key that unlocks much of the first chapter of John's Gospel. For example, the Apostle John wrote: *"And the Word made flesh and dwelt among us..."* (John 1:14). John spoke of Jesus Christ, saying that He was made flesh and dwelt among us. It is this passage that reveals the true intent of the veil in the Tabernacle. The word "dwelt" in this passage means "to pitch a tent, to tabernacle." In W. Vines Expository Dictionary of New Testament Words, we read: "Skenoo, to pitch a tent, to tabernacle, is translated "dwelt" in John 1:14, A.V., R. V. marg., "tabernacled" And the Word was made flesh and set up His tabernacle in our midst." [1] God could have chosen many other words to express "dwelt" or "dwell," but He chose this one. This word usage expresses the mind of God concerning His incarnation. Christ tabernacled among us as God tabernacled among Israel in the wilderness. Just as the veil prevented the people from seeing God's Glory, the flesh and humanity of Jesus prevented people from seeing His deity during His earthly ministry.

The word "dwelt" in this passage reveals another significant truth. We read it in a quote from Adam Clarke's Commentary: John 1:14, "And Tabernacled among us: the human nature which he took of the Virgin, being as the shrine, house, or temple, in which his immaculate deity condescended to dwell. The word is probably an allusion to the Divine Shechinah in the Jewish temple, as God has represented the whole Gospel dispensation through the types and ceremonies of the Old Covenant; so the Shechinah in the Tabernacle and temple pointed to this manifestation of God in the flesh. The word is thus used by the Jewish writers: it signifies with them a manifestation of the Divine Shechinah. The original word signifies 1. to build a booth, tent, or temporary hut, for present shelter or convenience; and does not properly signify a lasting habitation or dwelling place; and is therefore fitly applied to the human nature of Christ, which like the Tabernacle of old, was to be here only for a temporary residence for the eternal Divinity." (2)

The word "dwelt" refers to a "temporary shelter" for "convenience." Jesus Christ's body housed the presence of God just as the Tabernacle in the wilderness did! And, as the Tabernacle in the Wilderness was only a temporary dwelling for God's glory, Jesus' body was also only a **temporary dwelling place for God**. The writer of Colossians said it this way, *"For in Him dwelleth all the fullness of the Godhead bodily."* (Colossians 2:9). This insight raises a question. If Jesus Christ was truly God incarnate, why isn't it evident in the Gospels? The answer to the question is found in the "veil." A veil hid God's presence in the Tabernacle in the wilderness, and a "veil" hid Jesus' deity during His earthly ministry. In referring to the believer's access to God today, the Bible states: *"By a new and living way, which he hath consecrated for us, through the veil, that is to say, his flesh."* (Hebrews 10:20). Here, we read the flesh of Jesus Christ was the "veil" that hid His deity! The

Apostle Paul wrote: *"To wit, that God was in Christ, reconciling the world unto himself, not imputing their trespasses unto them; and hath committed unto us the word of reconciliation."* (2 Corinthians 5:19).

Before His crucifixion and resurrection, Jesus did not want others (except those close to him, i.e., his disciples) to know He was God. Even when He performed mighty miracles, He often charged those involved, including a multitude on one occasion (Matthew 12:16), to remain silent. The following are instances where Jesus commanded the people to remain silent regarding their healing:

Leper healed Matthew 8:4, Luke 5: 14

A blind man was healed in Matthew 9:30

Multitude healed Matthew 12:16

When Peter called him the Christ, Matthew 16:15-20, Mark 8:30

12-year-old girl healed Mark 5:43

The Transfiguration Matthew 17:9

Unclean Spirits called him Son of God, Mark 3:11-12

Peter, James, and John witnessed the vision of the Transfiguration where Jesus spoke to Moses and Elijah *"... and a voice out of the cloud, which said, 'This is my beloved Son, in whom I am well pleased."* Jesus tells these three men not to speak of these things until after his resurrection:

"And as they came down from the mountain, Jesus charged them, saying, Tell the vision to no man, until the Son of man be risen again from the dead." (Matthew 17:9). After they crucified Jesus, the veil in the Temple was "rent" torn in two (Matthew 27:50-51a). The tearing of the veil signified the way to God was no longer hidden or restricted to priests. Something else occurred following Jesus' resurrection: the Apostles addressed Jesus as "God." (John 20:28). When the "veil" was "rent," it opened the way for believers to approach God and fully revealed the true nature of Jesus Christ, God incarnate.

Just before his crucifixion, Phillip asks Jesus to show them the Father: *"Jesus saith unto him, Have I been so long time with you, and yet hast thou not known me, Philip? he that hath seen me hath seen the Father; and how sayest thou then, Shew us the Father?"* (John 14:9). Following Christ's resurrection, He appears among the Apostles. The Apostle Thomas doubted that it was Jesus. But when he saw the wounds in Christ's hands and His side, he exclaimed, *"My Lord and my God"* (John 20:28). Paul, writing to Titus, wrote: *"Looking for that blessed hope and the glorious appearing of the great God and our Saviour Jesus Christ."* (Titus 2:13). The "veil" had been removed, torn, and the whole nature of Jesus Christ, as God, incarnate, was revealed. His Jewish disciples understood this. Jesus told them that a time would come when He would reveal the Father, *"I have told you these things in parables (veiled language, allegories, dark sayings). The hour is now coming when I shall no longer speak to you in figures of speech, but*

I shall tell you about the Father in plain words and openly without reserve." (John 16:15 - Amplified Bible). His deity was a secret, veiled, until the appointed time. But when the prophetic calendar was fulfilled, then the veil was removed.

Remember, Jesus expressly prohibited the disciples from revealing His identity prematurely. *"When Jesus came into the coasts of Caesarea Philippi, he asked his disciples, saying, Whom do men say that I the Son of man am?... Thou art the Christ, the Son of the living God. And Jesus answered and said unto him, Blessed art thou, Simon Barjona: for flesh and blood hath not revealed it unto thee, but my Father which is in heaven ... Then charged he his disciples that they should tell no man that he was Jesus the Christ."* (Matthew 16:13-20).

During Jesus' public ministry, He did not openly claim to be God. But it would be incorrect to say Jesus never claimed to be God. Jesus used Old Testament figures and passages of scripture to reveal His identity to His Jewish listeners during His ministry. In John 5:18, He called God His "father." His listeners understood what He meant *"But Jesus answered them, My Father worketh hitherto, and I work. Therefore the Jews sought the more to kill him, because he not only had broken the sabbath but said also that God was his Father, making himself equal with God."* In John 8:56, Jesus claimed to see Abraham, *"Your father Abraham rejoiced to see my day: and he saw it and was glad."* The Jews *"... took up stones to cast at him: but Jesus hid himself, and went out of the temple, going through the midst of them, and so passed by."* The reason they tried to stone Jesus is found in His words, *"Then said the Jews unto him, Thou art not yet fifty years old, and hast thou seen Abraham? Jesus said unto them, Verily, verily, I say unto you, Before Abraham was, **I am**."* (John 8:57-58). The Jews knew Jesus claimed to be the great "I AM." I AM is the name God gave to Moses (Exodus 3:14). In John 10:30-33, Jesus said, *"I and my Father are one. Then the Jews took up stones again to stone him. Jesus answered them, Many good works have I shewed you from my Father; for which of those works do ye stone me? The Jews answered him, saying, For a good work we stone thee not; but for blasphemy; and because that thou, being a man, makest thyself God."* They understood!

Besides the previous three attempts on His life, there were four more. The first occurred after His birth. King Herod heard a "King of the Jews" had been born in Bethlehem. He did not know his birth date, so he ordered the murder of all male children born in Bethlehem, two years old and under. (Matthew 2:16). The second attempt occurred thirty years later when Jesus began His public ministry; Jesus was led into the wilderness to pray and fast. After 40 days, the devil tried to kill Him, saying, *"If you are the Son of God, throw yourself down from here..."* (Luke 4:9-12). Following His temptation in the wilderness, Jesus returned to His hometown of Nazareth. It was here, in Nazareth, where the next attempt on his life would occur. While in Nazareth, He went to the Synagogue and read a Messianic prophecy from Isaiah (61:1). Luke tells us what happened, *"And all they in the synagogue, when they heard these things, were filled with wrath, And rose up, and thrust him out of the city, and led him unto the brow of the hill whereon their city was built, that they might cast him down headlong. But he passing through the midst of them went his way,"* (Luke 4:28-30). The final attempt proved "successful," it was His crucifixion (Mark 15). He knew they would kill Him. But it would be at the time appointed by God. *"Then Jesus said unto them, My time is not yet come: but your time is alway ready. The world cannot hate you; but me it hateth, because I testify of it, that the works thereof are evil. Go ye up unto this feast: I go not up yet unto this feast; for my time is not yet full come."* (John 7:6-8). He knew when His time had come: *"And he cometh the third time, and saith unto them, Sleep on now, and take your rest: it is enough, the hour is come; behold, the Son of man is betrayed into the hands of sinners."* (Mark 14:41).

They did kill Jesus at the appointed time and place. Though it appeared to be a victory for the enemy, it was not. In crucifying the Messiah, the enemy unwittingly helped usher in the age of grace. Here is what the apostle Paul wrote: *"But we speak the wisdom of God in a mystery, even the hidden wisdom, which God ordained before the world unto our glory: Which none of the princes of this world knew: for had they known it, they would not have crucified the Lord of glory."* (1 Corinthians 2:7-8). When the crucifixion was accomplished, the "veil" was removed for all time, and the glory of God, God in Christ, was made manifest to the entire world. His primary mission was not to assert His deity (Philippians 2:6) but to proclaim salvation and establish the Kingdom of God. Had He made His deity the focal point instead of His message of salvation and the restoration of the Kingdom of God, it would have led to His premature death. He knew this.

From Genesis to Revelation, we read God's desire to be with and among His people. In the Garden of Eden, the Tabernacle in the wilderness, the Temple in Israel, and now through the presence of Jesus Christ, through the Holy Spirit, God desires to tabernacle, to tent with and be among His people. And so it is with that thought that we read this scripture from the last book of the Bible, *"And I heard a great voice out of heaven saying, Behold, the tabernacle of God is with men, and he will dwell with them, and they shall be his people, and God himself shall be with them, and be their God."* (Revelations 21:3).

The Form of God

" In your relationships with one another, have the same mindset as Christ Jesus: Who, being in very nature God, did not consider equality with God something to be used to his own advantage;" (Philippians 2:6 NIV). This passage explains why Jesus kept His deity veiled during His earthly ministry. In 2010, The Committee on Bible Translation determined: "When the NIV was first translated, the meaning of the rare Greek word harpagmos, rendered "something to be grasped," in Philippians 2:6 was uncertain. But further study has shown that the word refers to **something that a person has in their possession but**

chooses not to use to their advantage. The updated New International Version reflects this added information, making clear that Jesus was equal with God when he determined to become a human for our sake: "[Christ Jesus], being in very nature God, did not consider equality with God something to be used to his advantage." Continuing, we read: *"but emptied himself, taking the form of a servant, being made in the likeness of men; and being found in fashion as a man, he humbled himself, becoming obedient even unto death, yea, the death of the cross."* (Philippians 2:7-8). (www.thewordbooks.com/index.php/product/new-international-version-2011/). Jesus took the title "Son of Man" upon Himself during His earthly ministry.

This scripture points out that God, in his essence and nature, took upon himself the flesh of a man, a servant who was the human, visible body of Jesus Christ. This, however, did not mean that he left all his glory or nature in heaven, but instead brought it to earth, disguised or hidden by his flesh, as the scripture reveals in Hebrews 10:20, which was the "veil." We know that he did not leave his essence or nature in heaven because Colossians 2:9 tells us all the fulness of the Godhead dwelt bodily in Jesus Christ.

Footnotes Chapter 11

1. W. E. Vines Expository Dictionary of New Testament Words, page 345, Revell 1966

2. Adam Clarke's Commentary John 1:14

Chapter 12
Two Witnesses Speak

"For precept must be upon precept, precept upon precept; line upon line, line upon line; here a little, and there a little." Isaiah 28:10.

In the following scriptures, I took an Old Testament (OT) description or characteristic of God and showed Jesus has the same exclusive attribute or characteristic in the New testament(NT).

Savior

OT *"I, even I, am the LORD (YHWH); and beside me there is no saviour."* Isaiah 43:11.

NT *"For unto you is born this day in the city of David a Saviour, which is Christ the Lord."* Luke 2:11

Creator

OT *"In the beginning, God created the heaven and the earth."* Genesis 1:1

NT *"For by him were all things created, that are in heaven, and that are in earth, visible and invisible, whether they be thrones, or dominions, or principalities, or powers: all things were created by him, and for him:"* Colossians 1:16

Lord of Lords

OT *"For the LORD your God is God of gods, and Lord of lords, a great God, a mighty, and a terrible, which regardeth not persons, nor taketh reward:"* Deuteronomy 10:17

NT *"And he hath on his vesture and on his thigh a name written, KING OF KINGS, AND LORD OF LORDS."* Revelation 19:16 Acts 10:36

"I AM"

OT *"And God said unto Moses, I AM THAT I AM: and he said, Thus shalt thou say unto the children of Israel, I AM hath sent me unto you."* Ex. 3:14

NT *"I tell you in solemn truth,"* returned Jesus, *"before there was an Abraham, I AM!"* John 8:58 (J.B. Phillips)

The Pierced One

OT *"And I will pour upon the house of David, and upon the inhabitants of Jerusalem, the spirit of grace and of supplications: and they shall look upon me whom they have pierced, and they shall mourn for him, as one mourneth for his only son,...* Zech. 12:10

NT *"Behold, he cometh with clouds; and every eye shall see him, and they also which pierced him: and all kindreds of the earth shall wail because of him. Even so, Amen."* Revelation 1:7

God

OT *"The voice of him that crieth in the wilderness, Prepare ye the way of the LORD, make straight in the desert a highway for our God."* Isaiah 40:3

NT *"The beginning of the gospel of Jesus Christ, the Son of God; As it is written in the prophets, Behold, I send my messenger before thy face, which shall prepare thy way before thee. The voice of one crying in the wilderness, Prepare ye the way of the Lord, make his paths straight."* Mark 1:1-3

Almighty God

OT *"And when Abram was ninety years old and nine, the LORD appeared to Abram and said unto him, I am the Almighty God; walk before me, and be thou perfect."* Genesis 17:1

NT *"I am Alpha and Omega, the beginning and the ending, saith the Lord, which is, and which was, and which is to come, the Almighty."* Revelation 1:8

The Shepherd

OT *"The LORD is my shepherd; I shall not want."* Psalm 23:1

NT *"I am the good shepherd, and know my sheep, and am known of mine."* John 10:14

Every Knee Will Bow

OT *"Look unto me, and be ye saved, all the ends of the earth: for I am God, and there is none else. I have sworn by myself, the word is gone out of my mouth in righteousness, and shall not return, That unto me every knee shall bow, every tongue shall swear."* Isaiah 45:22-23

NT *"That at the name of Jesus every knee should bow, of things in heaven, and things in earth, and things under the earth; And that every tongue should confess that Jesus Christ is Lord, to the glory of God the Father."* Philippians 2:10-11

The Holy One

OT *"I will also praise thee with the psaltery, even thy truth, O my God: unto thee will I sing with the harp, O thou Holy One of Israel."* Psalms 71:22

NT *"But ye denied the Holy One and the Just and desired a murderer to be granted unto you;"* Acts 3:14

Omnipresent

OT *"Can any hide in secret places that I shall not see him? saith the LORD. Do not I fill heaven and earth? saith the LORD."* Jeremiah 23:24

NT *"Teaching them to observe all things whatsoever I have commanded you: and, lo, I am with you alway, even unto the end of the world. Amen."* Matthew 28:20

Omniscient

OT *"Great is our Lord, and of great power: his understanding is infinite."* Psalms 147:5

NT *"In whom are hid all the treasures of wisdom and knowledge."* Colossians 2:3

Omnipotent

OT *"God hath spoken once; twice have I heard this; that power belongeth unto God."* Psalms 62:11

NT *"And Jesus came and spake unto them, saying, All power is given unto me in heaven and in earth."* Matthew 28:18

Self-Existent

OT *"Who hath wrought and done it, calling the generations from the beginning? I the LORD, the first, and with the last; I am he."* Isaiah 41:4

NT *"I am Alpha and Omega, the beginning and the ending, saith the Lord, which is, and which was, and which is to come, the Almighty."* Revelation 1:8

Bridegroom

OT *"For as a young man marrieth a virgin, so shall thy sons marry thee: and as the bridegroom rejoiceth over the bride, so shall thy God rejoice over thee."* Isaiah 62:5

NT *"And Jesus said unto them, Can the children of the bridechamber fast, while the bridegroom is with them? as long as they have the bridegroom with them, they cannot fast."* Mark 2:19

Redeemer (Purchaser)

OT *"I will ransom them from the power of the grave; I will redeem them from death: O death, I will be thy plagues; O grave, I will be thy destruction: repentance shall be hid from mine eyes."* Hosea 13:14

NT *"Christ hath redeemed us from the curse of the law, being made a curse for us: for it is written, Cursed is everyone that hangeth on a tree:"* Galatians 3:13

Judge

OT *"Let the heathen be wakened and come up to the valley of Jehoshaphat: for there will I sit to judge all the heathen round about."* Joel 3:12

NT *"When the Son of man shall come in his glory, and all the holy angels with him, then shall he sit upon the throne of his glory:"* Matthew 25:3

In some Old Testament passages mentioned above, an attribute or characteristic of God is exclusive, e.g., "no other Saviour" (Isaiah 43:11). However, in the New Testament, Jesus Christ is called the Saviour (Luke 2:11). There is not a second Saviour. The other example is Isaiah 45:22-23, *"... for I am God, and there is none else... That unto me every knee shall bow, every tongue shall swear."* In the New Testament, every knee will bow to Jesus Christ: *"That at the name of Jesus every knee should bow, of things in heaven, and things in earth, and things under the earth;"* (Philippians 2:10-11). These and other scriptures reveal the real nature of Jesus Christ. He is the great God incarnate.

Chapter 13

The Mystery of the Name

"What is His name, or His son's name if thou canst tell."
Proverbs 30:4

His father gave him only one name. But history changed that. While his father was a King, the son distinguished himself in other ways. He never lost a battle. History records no retreats. His armies were destined to rule the world. And they did, from the coast of Africa to India. In fact, through his efforts, the East merged with the West for the first time in history. His influence was so significant that an era of history, Hellenism, began because of his many conquests. Tragedy struck at the age of 33. He became sick, and within two short weeks, he lay dead. For the next fifty years, his generals fought among themselves to control the empire he left behind. All the while, he lay wrapped in gold in a glass coffin on display in the city named after him. They call the city Al-Iskandarijah in Arabic, but you know the city as Alexandria and the man as Alexander the Great.

This took place over 2000 years ago. Had I revealed his name first, you would have known about him. Why? Because names, not only facts and history, are important. In the Bible, names are important too. Names were given to reflect a characteristic. Sometimes God would change a name. For example, we read about a man who wrestled with an angel of God. His name was Jacob, whose name means "to supplant" or "follow after." Jacob prevailed and asked for a blessing. What blessing did God give him? God changed his name to "Israel." That was the blessing. Israel means "ruling with God." God also changed Abram's name to Abraham and Sarai's to Sarah. Jesus changed Simon's name to Peter. Luke changed Saul's name to Paul in chronicling his journeys and work. Names are important, and none more important than God's name. The Name of God in the Old Testament comprises four consonants YHWH. Therefore, God's Name is known as the Nomen Tetragrammaton or the Name of Four Letters. Those are the letters in the Hebrew language that spell the Name of God.

One of the ten commandments of God dealt with this name: *"thou shalt not take the name of the LORD (YHWH) thy God in vain for the LORD (YHWH) will not hold him guiltless that taketh his name in vain."* (Exodus 20:7). Because of this commandment, the Hebrews feared using God's name "in vain." Only the High Priest could speak the Name, and he only once a year. Instead of speaking or writing the Name, they replaced it with the word Adonai (Hebrew), translated as Kyrios in Greek and Lord in English. Every time the Name of God appeared in the Septuagint without the definite article, the translators put the word "Kyrios" in its place. It is interesting to note that Jesus even upheld the practice of not speaking the "Name of Four Letters." When Jesus spoke of God while he was here, He used the same word that the Jews used, "Adonai" or Lord.

A popular word for God today is Jehovah. Many people, including Christians, have embraced this word in place of The Name YHWH. The word Jehovah appears in many translations of the Bible, and it is used by many scholars, writers, and commentators. All of this gives this word, Jehovah, a sense of legitimacy. My first observation is this: the word Jehovah does not appear in any Hebrew or Greek manuscripts. It could not have appeared in any Hebrew or Greek manuscripts. Why? The Hebrew language does not have the necessary vowels to create the word Jehovah. If there are no vowels in the Hebrew alphabet, one could be prompted to ask, "where did this word, Jehovah, come from?" The Encyclopedia Britannica explains the creation of this word: "Jehovah (Yahweh), in the Bible, the God of Israel. "Jehovah" is a modern mispronunciation of the Hebrew name, resulting from combining the consonants of that name, Jhvh, with the vowels of the word ădōnāy, "Lord," which the Jews substituted for the proper name in reading the scriptures." (1)

If you take the four consonants from the Hebrew YHWH and add the vowels from the word ădōnāy together, they create the word "Jehovah." Here is how it was created:

Y H W H (Nomen Tetragrammaton)

  A   O   A (add the vowels taken from ădōnāy)

YAHOWAH   (added together, they spell Yahowah)

We can only speculate about the NAME's correct pronunciation, even with the added vowels. That doesn't stop the Witnesses. The Witnesses changed Yahowah to Jehovah and put it in their NWT of the Bible. The first clue that the word "Jehovah" is incorrect is that the Hebrew alphabet does not have a "J." The letter "J" is substituted for the letter "Y." The "J" came from the German translation with the "J" replacing the Hebrew letter "Y" sound. An interesting historical fact sheds additional light on the creation of the word Jehovah. In the English language, the letter "J" was not added until the seventeenth century. Before that time, the letter "I" was used. The word Jehovah could not have appeared in any English translations of the Bible before this time. As I have said, it is a manufactured word. It is not a proper name for God.

I contend that changing the Name of God has led to an error in understanding the incarnation and deity of Jesus Christ. One religious group that is the leading proponent of using the word Jehovah is the Jehovah's Witnesses. They use this word, Jehovah, to obscure the deity of Jesus Christ throughout their New World Translation of the Bible (see chapter six, "Is Jesus God or "a god?"")

In their New World Translation, they claim they substituted the word Jehovah where "theos" (God) and "Kurios" (Lord) appear in the text. The problem is this; they do not follow their own rule. As an example, they did not translate "Lord" as "Jehovah" when Thomas referred to the Lord Jesus Christ as "my Lord and my God" in John 20:28-29: *"And Thomas answered and said unto him, My Lord and my God. Jesus saith unto him, Thomas, because thou hast seen me, thou hast believed: blessed are they that have not seen, and yet have believed."* In this passage, Thomas called Jesus "Lord" and "God." If the New World Translation had followed their guidelines, it would have translated the word "Lord" as Jehovah. However, if they did that, it would be a tacit admission that Jesus Christ is God incarnate. They insist Jesus is "a god," so they did not substitute "Jehovah" for "Lord" in translating this passage.

They are merely attempting to reinforce their belief that Jesus Christ is a "god" and not God incarnate. They have altered other passages of scripture. In these alterations, the Witnesses are clearly attempting to depict Jesus Christ as "a god." If they faithfully translated the scriptures, they would have to acknowledge the full nature of Jesus Christ, the God/Man. Despite their attempt to obscure Jesus' deity, the scriptures declare His deity when properly understood. The following is a list of Old Testament Names for God, in which the Name YHWH was used in describing an attribute of God. We find the same attributes applied to Jesus Christ in the New Testament.

In the Old Testament, God was known by "compound names." A compound name would include The Name YHWH followed by a descriptive title: e.g., YHWH Yireh, which means "the LORD will provide." The following is a list of compound names for God in the Old Testament:

The Compound Names

YHWH-Jireh (Genesis 22:13-14) — The LORD will provide

YHWH-Rapha (Exodus 15:26) — The LORD that healeth

YHWH-Nissi (Exodus 17:8-15) — The LORD our Banner

YHWH-Shalom (Judges 6:24) — The LORD our Peace

YHWH-Ra-ah Shepherd (Psalm 23:1) — The LORD is the Way, my

YHWH-Tsidkenu (Jeremiah 23:6) — The LORD our Righteousness

YHWH-Shammah (Ezekiel 48:35, Micah 7:8) — The LORD is the Light, ever-present

YHWH Mekaddishkem (Ex. 31:13) — The LORD that sanctifies thee

YHWH Sabaoth	The LORD of Hosts (1 Sam. 1:3)
YHWH Elyon	The LORD most high (Ps. 7:17)

Of interest to us is that these compound names that identified the LORD (YHWH) in the Old Testament apply to Jesus Christ in the New Testament. These are additional proofs of the deity of Jesus Christ. Here is the list in the New Testament:

The Lord will provide	John 1:29
The Lord that healeth	Matt. 10:8
The Lord our banner	John 12:32
The Lord our peace	Eph. 2:13-14
The Lord our shepherd	John 10:11
The Lord our righteousness	1 Cor. 1:30
The Lord is our light	John 1:9 (John 8:12)
The Lord is present,	Matt. 28:20
The Lord that sanctifies thee	1 Cor. 1:30
The Lord of Hosts	Rev. 19:11-14
The Lord Most High	Phil 2:9

These provide another textual proof of the deity of Jesus Christ.

One Name

The prophet Zechariah wrote: *"And the LORD shall be king over all the earth: in that day shall there be one LORD, and his name one."* (Zechariah 14:9). Zechariah was writing about the last days in this passage. He prophesied in those days; God's name would be one. When did the last days begin? They began on the day of Pentecost following the resurrection of Jesus. The Apostle Peter stood up on the day of Pentecost and said that these are the "last days." Here is what Peter said: *"But this is that which was spoken by the prophet Joel; And it shall come to pass in the last days, saith God, I will pour out of my Spirit upon all flesh: and your sons and your daughters shall prophesy, and your young men shall see visions, and your old men shall dream dreams...."* (Acts 2:16-17).

The early disciples embraced the name of Jesus Christ. This is significant when we consider they were all Jews. At one point, they were forbidden to preach "in the name of Jesus Christ." *"But when they had commanded them to go aside out of the council, they conferred among themselves, Saying, What shall we do to these men? for that indeed a notable miracle hath been done by them is manifest to all them that dwell in Jerusalem, and we cannot deny it. But that it spread no further among the people, let us straightly threaten them, that they speak henceforth to no man in this name. And they called them and commanded them not to speak at all nor teach in the name of Jesus. But Peter and John answered and said unto them, Whether it be right in the sight of God to hearken unto you more than unto God, judge ye. For we cannot but speak the things which we have seen and heard."* (Acts 4:15-20). Despite the threat, they continued to teach/preach in Jesus' name.

It is interesting to note that the Apostles could have taught or preached in any other name except the name of the Lord Jesus Christ. They did not. They preached in His name, were baptized in His name, and changed countless lives, all in the name of the Lord Jesus Christ. In one instance, the apostles healed a man in the name of Jesus. The Apostles were asked, *"By what power or what name have you done this?"* (Acts 4:7). The Apostles had a choice: which was it, a power or a name? The Apostle Peter answered: *"Be it known unto you all and to all the people of Israel that by the Name of Jesus Christ of Nazareth, whom you crucified, whom God raised from the dead, even by Him doth this man stand here before you whole."* (Acts 4:10). They did not shrink from the challenge, they made it known, *"by the name of Jesus Christ...this man stands before you whole."*

On the day of Pentecost, after the Holy Spirit fell upon the disciples, Peter stood up and preached Christ unto the Jews that had gathered in Jerusalem for the feast. When they asked what they must do to be saved, Peter replied: *"Then Peter said unto them, Repent, and be baptized every one of you in the name of Jesus Christ for the remission of sins, and ye shall receive the gift of the Holy Ghost."* (Acts 2:38). The only name ever used, in the scriptures, when baptizing new converts was Jesus'. (See Chapter 10, A Contradiction Resolved, for the complete biblical history of water baptisms) It is beyond dispute that the name given to the church, the name above every other name, is the Lord Jesus Christ: *"Wherefore God also hath highly exalted him and given him a name which is above every name:"* (Philippians 2:9).

The apostle Paul will have the final word: *"And whatsoever ye do in word or deed, do all in the name of the*

Lord Jesus, giving thanks to God and the Father by him." (Colossians 3:17).

Elohim

The Hebrew word Elohim appears in the Old Testament over 2500 times. Most often, it is translated as "God." It is also translated as "a god" or "gods", "demons", "angels", "kings" and "prophets". Elohim is a "plural noun." Because it is a "plural noun," some have concluded there is a plurality of persons in the Godhead. They see in the word "Elohim" support for the doctrine of the Trinity, i.e., three persons in the Godhead. Does the word Elohim support this belief?

There is a rule that governs the meaning of Elohim when it is translated as God in the Old Testament. The rule: "In Hebrew, the ending -im normally indicates a masculine plural. However, when referring to the Hebrew God, Elohim is usually understood to be grammatically singular (i.e., it governs a singular verb or adjective). In Modern Hebrew, it is often referred to in the singular despite the -im ending that denotes plural masculine nouns in Hebrew." (2)

To determine whether the word Elohim, in the Old Testament, is a "plural noun," we must look at the verb. The rule is used in the first verse of the Bible: *"In the beginning, God created the heaven and the earth."* (Genesis 1:1). This passage tells the reader God (Elohim, masculine plural) created (singular verb) the heaven and the earth. Thus, in this verse, Elohim is understood to be singular, not plural. If this passage lacked the verb "created," Elohim would have been translated as a plural; "gods." The rule tells us the verb determines whether the noun, Elohim, is plural or singular. For example, here is an instance in the Old Testament in which the word Elohim is correctly translated as a plural. In Exodus 20:3, we read a passage that recognizes the "plurality" of the suffix "im," *"thou shall have no other gods before me."* Notice the word "gods" (Elohim) is rendered in the plural. That is because no singular verb is connected to it; thus, it is correctly translated as "gods" and not God.

We also have an example in which the word "Elohim," applying to a pagan goddess, is to be understood as singular, not a plural. We read in 1 Kings 11:5: *"For Solomon went after Ashtoreth the goddess (Elohim) of the Zidonians and after Milcom the abomination of the Ammonites."* Notice the suffix attached to Ashtoreth, "eth." The "eth" suffix, in Hebrew, is for a "singular feminine noun," though this goddess' name (Elohim) is in the masculine plural. The International Standard Encyclopedia states: "From Babylonia, the worship of the goddess was carried to the Semites of the West, and in most instances, they attached the feminine suffix to her name (eth); where this was not the case, they regarded the deity as a male." (3). She was the goddess (Elohim), not the "goddesses" of the Zidonians.

The word Elohim is also applied to various gods of the pagan world in the Old Testament. Here are a few examples: The god Baalberith: *"And it came to pass, as soon as Gideon was dead, that the children of Israel turned again, and went a whoring after Baalim, and made Baalberith their god (Elohim)."* (Judges 8:33). The god Chemosh: *"wilt not thou possess that which Chemosh thy god (Elohim) giveth thee to possess? So whomsoever the LORD our God shall drive out from before us, them will we possess."* (Judges 11:24). The god Dagon: *"Then the lords of the Philistines gathered them together for to offer a great sacrifice unto Dagon their god (Elohim), and to rejoice: for they said, Our god (Elohim) hath delivered Samson our enemy into our hand."* (Judges 16:23, see also (Marduk, Daniel 1:2, Milcom, 1 Kings 11:3, Baal, 1 Kings 18::24 and Baal-Zebub 2 Kings 1:2).

These pagan gods are addressed as Elohim. However, none of them were trinities of three persons. This demonstrates, again, that the word "Elohim" does not require it to be understood as a "plural noun." Recalling the rule, the verb, if one is in the text, determines whether it is plural or singular.

The scriptures use other "plural nouns," words in Hebrew that have the "im" suffix but are singular e.g.

shamayim = sky

mayim = water

panim = face

Baalim = Husband, Master (Isaiah 54:5)

Morim = Teacher (Isaiah 30:20)

Osim = Maker (Isaiah 54:5, Psalms 118:7; 149:2, Job 35:10)

Kedoshim = Holy One (Hosea 12:1, Proverbs 9:10; 30:3)

Finally, Moses, a single man, is called "Elohim" in the scriptures (Exodus 7:1)

Elohim In The New Testament

The translation of the Hebrew Old Testament into Greek is known as the Septuagint. The word Septuagint is Latin, meaning "seventy." It is abbreviated as LXX, which are Roman numerals for the number seventy. Tradition tells us seventy Jewish scholars (or 72) were chosen to translate the Hebrew scriptures into Koine Greek between 300-200 BC. At the time of Christ, the Jewish people spoke both Aramaic and Greek. Aramaic was the dominant language of the Jews, while Greek was the language of the empire. The New Testament writers penned the various letters in Koine Greek, though they were all Jews, except Luke.

When the Septuagint was translated from Hebrew into Greek, the translators used the Greek "Theos" (God) for the Hebrew word "Elohim." They also used the Greek word "Kyrios" for the Hebrew word "Adonai" (Lord). As an example, we read in the Hebrew text: *"In the beginning, God (Elohim) created the heavens and the earth."* (Genesis 1:1). Here is the same verse in Greek: *"In the beginning, God (Theos) made the heavens and the earth."* (Genesis 1:1).

Often, when the writers of the New Testament quoted from the Old Testament, they chose the Septuagint version, instead of the Hebrew, for their source. As an example, Luke writes in the New Testament book of Acts: *"The God (Theos) of Abraham, and of Isaac, and of Jacob, the God (Theos) of our fathers, hath glorified his Son Jesus; whom ye delivered up, and denied him in the presence of Pilate, when he was determined to let him go."* (Acts 3:13). Luke is quoting Exodus 3:6: *"Moreover he said, I am the God (Elohim) of thy father, the God (Elohim) of Abraham, the God (Elohim) of Isaac, and the God (Elohim) of Jacob. And Moses hid his face; for he was afraid to look upon God (Elohim)."* Note Luke's use of the Greek word "Theos," where "Elohim" appears in Exodus. We know the word "Elohim" is singular in the passage Luke quotes from Exodus. Thus, it would be reasonable to conclude that Luke used "Theos" here as a singular noun, not a plural. (See also Acts 5:30-31; 13:17; 17:24). Further support for using the

Septuagint version is this fact: Jesus quoted from the Septuagint translation several times: Heb 10:5-7, Ps 40:6-8, Is. 29:13, Mk 7:6-8, Mt 21:16, Matt 1:2, Is 7:14. In using the Greek word "Theos," where "Elohim" appeared in the Hebrew text, we know the translators equated the Greek word "Theos" with the Hebrew word "Elohim." In doing this, they tacitly acknowledged the Greek word "Theos," when referring to God, was to be understood as a "singular" noun, just as Elohim was in the original Hebrew language.

There are passages in the New Testament where Theos may be understood as either God or gods. This is because Greek has no word for "gods," plural. To distinguish between the singular and plural use, the translators added an article "ho" (the) before the singular use of Theos. E.W. Bullinger writes: "Theos..." however, having lost the meaning of the one God came to mean "a God" only, one of the many gods. Hence it became necessary in the New Testament to distinguish it by the article, "ho Theos, the one supreme with whom is the fountain of life and light...." He continues: "θεός is used without the article, and denotes the conception of God, as an Infinite and perfect Being, one who is almighty, infinite and, etc.., with the article ὁ θεός denotes the God, the revealed God, the God of the Bible, and according to the context may denote, this God, our God, etc." (4) Strong's Concordance has this entry under "Theos": #2316: "theos: a deity, figuratively, a magistrate. Especially (when used with #3588, the definite article "Ho"): the supreme Divinity; by Hebraism, very God [Almighty God, YHWH the Father of Jesus.]." When the article "ho" (the) precedes "Theos," it refers to the "Almighty God, YHWH."

The Greek translators added the definite article "ho" (the) in their writings to distinguish the true God from a god, god, or gods, with one exception. It is found in 2 Corinthians 4:4: *"In whom the god (ho theos) of this world hath blinded the minds of them which believe not, lest the light of the glorious gospel of Christ, who is the image of God, should shine unto them."* In this passage, the words "the god" (ho theos) are understood in context. This "god" has blinded the minds of people to the gospel. The context tells the reader that "the god" here is not the one true God; he is the "god of this world," i.e., Satan. The writers of the New Testament also apply the word "Theos" to Jesus without the article "ho," e.g., *"Looking for that blessed hope, and the glorious appearing of the great God and our Saviour Jesus Christ;* (Titus 2:13). However, by applying Sharp's rule (see page 64), we know the "great God" is "our Saviour Jesus Christ," thus the article is unnecessary.

The Complete Word Study Dictionary writes: "While the writers of the New Testament did not, always, use the Greek article "ho" (the) when referring to Jesus Christ, John did use it in John 20:28: *"And Thomas answered and said unto him, My Lord and my God."* In the Greek translation, the article "ho" appears before "Lord" and "God." However, in translating this passage into English, the article "ho" (the) is replaced with the word "my." This was done to accommodate the English translation, where God is never referred to as "the God" unless He "belongs" to someone, e.g., "the God of Abraham, the God of Isaac and the God of Jacob...". (5)

Neither the Old Testament translators nor the New Testament writers recognized a "compound unity" or "plurality." Any attempt to associate the word "Elohim" or "ho Theos" with a trinity of three persons is not supported by the Hebrew or Greek languages. It should be remembered; that no truth was more deeply ingrained in the Jewish mind than this: *"Hear o' Israel: The LORD our God is one LORD"* (Deuteronomy 6:4). The commandment is restated in Mark 12:29: *"And Jesus answered him, The first of all the commandments is, Hear, O Israel; The Lord our God is one Lord:"* (See also Romans 3:30 and Ephesians 4:6).

The word "gods" appears six times in the New Testament: John 10:34-37, Acts 14:11, Acts 17:18, Acts 19:26, 1 Corinthians 8:5, and Galatians 4:8. It is the English translation of the Greek word "theos," i.e., God. It is translated as a plural when the verb or pronoun requires a plural, e.g., *"Jesus answered them, Is it not written in your law, I said, **Ye** are gods? If he called **them** gods, unto whom the word of God came, and the scripture cannot be broken;"*(John 10:35).

Footnotes Chapter 13

1. Encyclopedia Britannica, 1911 Encyclopedia Britannica/Jehovah, Vol 15

2. Glinert, Modern Hebrew: An Essential Grammar, Routledge, p. 14, section 13 (b) Agreement

3. The International Standard Encyclopedia, page 271

4. A Critical Lexicon and Concordance to the English and Greek New Testament, pg. 331-332, E.W. Bullinger, Zondervan 1976

5. Zodhiates, Spiros, The Complete Word Study Dictionary: New Testament, AMG Publishers, 1992, pg. 730

Chapter 14

The Lord He Is God

"Unto thee it was shewed, that thou mightest know that the LORD he is God; there is none else beside him."
Deuteronomy 4:35

The word Lord has a remarkable history and meaning that may not be understood in the Christian community today. In a previous chapter, I mentioned the Tetragrammaton, YHWH. The Tetragrammaton appears in the Old Testament over 6800 times. Jews regard it as The Name of God. At some time in Israel's history, Jews stopped speaking the Tetragrammaton, though they continued to write it in the sacred text: "Rabbinical Judaism teaches that the name is forbidden to all except the High Priest, who should only speak it in the Holy of Holies of the Temple in Jerusalem on Yom Kippur. He then pronounces the name "just as it is written. As each blessing was made, the people in the courtyard were to prostrate themselves completely as they heard it spoken aloud. As the Temple has not been rebuilt since its destruction in 70 AD, most modern Jews never pronounce YHWH but instead read Adonai ("My Lord") during prayer and while reading the Torah and as HaShem ("The Name") at other times." [1] However, some believe the prohibition came about due to a strict interpretation of the commandment in Exodus 20:7: *"Thou shalt not take the name of the LORD thy God in vain; for the LORD will not hold him guiltless that taketh his name in vain."* This commandment refers to using God's Name when making a vow. Nothing in this commandment prohibits speaking The Name. The prohibition became, over time, a custom among the Jews. Following the destruction of the Temple in Jerusalem in 70 A.D., coupled with the prohibition to speak The Name, it fell into disuse. When The Name, YHWH, appeared in the Hebrew Old Testament, the Jews, out of reverence for The Name, would say "Adonai." Adonai means "Lord" in Hebrew.

When the Old Testament was translated into Greek (the Septuagint), they did not translate or transliterate The Name YHWH. They kept the Hebrew letters YHWH in the manuscript. This practice continued into the 4th century. Beginning in the 4th century, "the most complete copies" used the word Kyrios (Greek for Lord) or Theos (Greek for God) to replace The Name in the text. From the Greek, they translated the scriptures into Latin, German, and other languages. The Septuagint (Greek) Old Testament's English translation used all capitals, "LORD," where The Name YHWH appeared. When the word "Lord" (standard capitalization) appears in the Old Testament, it refers to God's strength or sovereignty as owner and master, not YHWH's name. While the word Adonai may mean "lord" or "master," YHWH always meant the God of Israel. In the Greek translation, the Hebrew "Adonai" is rendered "Kyrios." Young's Literal Translation renders the word "Kyrios" as "Lord 667, lord 54, master 11, and sir six times". The Hebrew word Adonai, when translated into Greek as "Kyrios," is always used in the singular when referring to Jesus Christ as God.

When the New Testament was translated into English, the translators used the standard capitalization" Lord" instead of the capitalized "LORD" used in the English translation of the Old Testament, where "LORD" would have been correct. Unfortunately, using the lowercase "Lord" in passages where "LORD" would have been correct obscured the Lord's deity in the New Testament. (The exceptions are found in Matthew 22:24, Mark 12:36, Luke 20:42, Acts 2:34, and Rev. 19:16).

The question I would pose is this: "Is the name (YHWH) ever used in referring to Jesus in the New Testament?" The answer is yes. We find complementary quotes from both the Old and New Testaments that contain the name YHWH.

In Genesis 17:1, the English translation has The Name YHWH as LORD: *"And when Abram was ninety years old, and nine, the LORD (YHWH) appeared to Abram and said unto him, I am the Almighty God (Shadday); walk before me and be thou perfect."* (Genesis 17:1). What I want to point out is this; in this passage, YHWH is identified as the "Almighty God." If Jesus is called the "Almighty God" in the New Testament, then one could rightly conclude that The Name YHWH could be applied to Him.

We find the complementary passage in the New Testament book of Revelation that identifies Jesus as the Almighty: *"Behold, he cometh with clouds; and every eye shall see him, and they also which **pierced him**: and all kindreds of the earth shall wail because of him. Even so, Amen. I am Alpha and Omega, the beginning and the ending, saith the Lord, which is, and which was, and **which is to come**, the Almighty."* (Revelation 1:7-8). In this passage, the "Almighty" has been" pierced" and is "to come."

In Revelation 4:8, we read: *"And the four beasts had each of them six wings about him, and they were full of eyes within: and they rest not day and night, saying, Holy, holy, holy, **Lord God Almighty**, which was, and is, **and is to come."*** Who is the "Lord," "God," the "Almighty" in these two passages? The text gives us two clues: the Lord God

Almighty would "come with clouds..." and He would be "pierced."

The question to be answered is who was "pierced" and who "is to come?" Whoever it is must be the Almighty God, whose Old Testament Name is YHWH.

The apostle Matthew answers the first question: "who is coming?": *"And then shall appear the sign of the Son of man in heaven: and then shall all the tribes of the earth mourn, and they shall see the Son of man coming in the clouds of heaven with power and great glory"* (Matthew 24:30). It is beyond doubt; this refers to Jesus Christ. Jesus Christ is going to return. The apostle John answers the second question; "who was pierced?" *"But one of the soldiers with a spear pierced his side, and forthwith came there out blood and water."* (John 19:34). (See also Matthew 24:30, 26:64, Mark 13:26, 14:62). This is a reference to the crucifixion of Jesus Christ. These passages confirm that Jesus is the Almighty God (YHWH). This should not surprise anyone, as Jesus Christ was known by His (Jewish) disciples as the Lord God Almighty.

The prophet Isaiah confirmed this when he wrote: *"Assemble yourselves and come; draw near together, ye that are escaped of the nations: they have no knowledge that set up the wood of their graven image and pray unto a god that cannot save. Tell ye, and bring them near; yea, let them take counsel together: who hath declared this from ancient time? who hath told it from that time? have not I the* **LORD (YHWH)***? and there is* **no God (El) else beside me***; a just God (El) and a* **Saviour***; there is none beside me***.** *Look unto me, and be ye saved, all the ends of the earth: for I am God (El), and* **there is none else***. I have sworn by myself, the word is gone out of my mouth in righteousness, and shall not* *return, That **unto me every knee shall bow, every tongue shall swear.*** " (Isaiah 45:20-23). In this passage, Isaiah mentions two characteristics of God (YHWH) that are exclusive: 1. "a Savior; there is none beside me…". 2." *for I am God, and there is none else.*" In Isaiah's mind, there is only one "Savior," one God, to whom "every knee shall bow, every tongue shall swear"; YHWH.

We learn in the New Testament that Jesus Christ is the Saviour as we read in Luke 2:11: *"For unto you is born this day in the city of David a Saviour, which is Christ the Lord."* The Samaritans also recognized Jesus as the "Saviour": *"And said unto the (Samaritan) woman, Now we believe, not because of thy saying: for we have heard him ourselves, and know that this is indeed the Christ, the Saviour of the world."* John 4:42 (see also Philippians 3:20, 1 Timothy 1:1, 2 Timothy 1:10). Jesus Christ is the one that Isaiah says, "every knee" will bow to: *"For it is written, As I live, saith the Lord, every knee shall bow to me, and every tongue shall confess to God."* (Romans 14:11). Admittedly, this passage does not mention Jesus. However, in Paul's letter to the Philippians, he wrote: *"Wherefore God also hath highly exalted him, and given him a name which is above every name: That at the name of Jesus every knee should bow, of things in heaven, and things in earth, and things under the earth; And that every tongue should confess that Jesus Christ is Lord, to the glory of God the Father."* (Philippians 2:9-11). When we read these New Testament passages together, we understand that the (only) Savior, the (one) God (YHWH) of Isaiah's prophecy, is identified as Jesus Christ.

The prophet Joel wrote: *"And it shall come to pass that whosoever shall call on the **name of the LORD (YHWH)** shall be delivered: for in mount Zion and in*

*Jerusalem shall be deliverance, as **the LORD (YHWH)** hath said, and in the remnant whom **the LORD (YHWH)** shall call."* (2:32). Notice the word "LORD" appears three times in this passage. LORD (all upper-case letters) is the English translation of The Name YHWH in the Hebrew Old Testament. On the day of Pentecost, the apostle Peter quoted Joel: *"And it shall come to pass, that whosoever shall call on **the name of the Lord** shall be saved."* (Acts 2:21). We know "who" Peter was referring to when he used the word "Lord" in this passage, it was Jesus Christ: *"Therefore let all the house of Israel know assuredly, that **God hath made that same Jesus, whom ye have crucified, both Lord and Christ.**"* (Acts 2:36). Peter recognized Jesus was the one Joel called YHWH. Peter would have known what Joel had written, and Peter would have understood the implications when he called Jesus Lord.

The apostle Paul reinforces this conclusion when he quotes the prophet Joel: *"For whosoever shall call upon the name of the Lord shall be saved."* (Romans 10:13). Who is the "Lord" Paul writes about in this passage? The answer is found in the text: *"That if thou shalt confess with thy mouth the Lord Jesus, and shalt believe in thine heart that God hath raised him from the dead, thou shalt be saved."* (Romans 10:9). These are "proof texts" that connect The Name YHWH, in the Old Testament with the Lord Jesus Christ in the New Testament.

Interestingly, the Jews of Jesus' day refused to call anyone Lord, even under the penalty of death. Gustav Deissman, a German Protestant theologian, wrote: "Soon after the destruction of Jerusalem (70 A.D.), Jewish rebels in Egypt, so Josephus tells us, refused to call the Caesar, Lord, because they held "God alone to be the Lord" — and died as martyrs, men and boys."[2] During the time of Christ, we read about Jewish men who died because they refused to call Caesar Lord! Though they refused to call Caesar Lord, these same Jews, who became believers in Jesus Christ, called Him Lord. We know the Apostles believed in the deity of Jesus Christ, as did the first church. And the majority of the early church fathers also believed in the deity of Jesus Christ: Ignatius (A.D. 50-117) writes: "For our God, Jesus the Christ, was conceived by Mary according to God's plan, both from the seed of David and of the Holy Spirit." [3] "I glorify Jesus Christ, the God who made you so wise, for I observed that you are established in an unshakable faith, having been nailed, as it were, to the cross of the Lord Jesus Christ."[4] Justin Martyr (A.D. 100-165) wrote: "Permit me first to recount the prophecies, which I wish to do to prove that Christ is called both God and Lord of hosts." [5] Irenaeus (A.D.130-202) wrote: "He received testimony from all that He was very man, and that He was very God, from the Father, from the Spirit, from angels, from the creation itself, from men, from apostate spirits and demons." [6] Irenaeus also wrote: "Carefully, then, has the Holy Ghost pointed out, by what has been said, His birth from a virgin, and His essence, that He is God (for the name Emmanuel indicates this). And He shows that He is a man .... [W]e should not understand that He is a mere man only, nor, on the other hand, from the name Emmanuel, should suspect Him to be God without flesh." [7] They were not alone: Clement of Alexandria (A.D. 150-215): "This Word, then, the Christ, the cause of both our being at first (for He was in God) and of our well-being, this very Word has now appeared as man, He alone being both, both God and man— the Author of all blessings to us; "[8] Tertullian (AD 150–225) wrote: "For God alone is without sin, and the only man without sin is Christ since Christ is also God." [9] Origen (AD 185–254) was another early Christian theologian.

Though he is reputed to have believed in "subordinationism," wrote: "Jesus Christ... in the last times, divesting Himself (of His glory), became a man, and was incarnate although God, and while made a man remained the God which He was." (10)

Footnotes on Chapter 14

1. Wikipedia, Names of God in Judaism, YHWH

2. Gustav Deissman, Light From the Ancient East, pg. 359

3. Ignatius, Letter to the Ephesians, 18.2

4. Ignatius, Letter to the Smyrnaeans, 1.1. Holmes, AF, 249

5. Justin Martyr, Dialogue with Trypho, 36. ANF, I:212

6. Irenaeus, Against Heresies, 4.6.7

7. Ibid 3.21.4

8. Clement of Alexander, Exhortation to the Heathen, 1

9. Tertullian, Treatise on the Soul, 41

10. Origen, De Principiis, Preface, 4

Chapter 15
The 1 John 5:7-8 Controversy

"For there are three that bear record in heaven, the Father, the Word, and the Holy Ghost: and these three are one. And there are three that bear witness in earth, the Spirit, and the water, and the blood: and these three agree in one." 1 John 5:7-8

This passage of scripture above has created controversy within the church. Some have used it to support their belief in three "persons" in the Godhead. Others claim the words are spurious and added later. The words in question are: *"the Father, the Word, and the Holy Ghost: and these three are one."* The New International Version renders this passage: *"For there are three that testify: the Spirit, the water and the blood; and the three are in agreement."* In this version, the words "the Father, the Word, and the Holy Ghost..." are absent. The Bible in Basic English has: *"And the Spirit is the witness because the Spirit is true. There are three witnesses, the Spirit, the water, and the blood: and all three are in agreement."* The Weymouth New Testament has: *"For there are three that give testimony — the Spirit, the water, and the blood; and there is complete agreement between these three."*

Many other Bible versions also recognize the spurious text and omit it. They include the New International Version, American Standard Version, New American Standard Bible, English Standard Version, New English Bible and Revised English Bible, New American Bible, Jerusalem Bible and New Jerusalem Bible, Good News Bible, New Living Translation, Holman Christian Standard Bible, Bible in Basic English and the Twentieth Century

New Testament. Dr. Neil Lightfoot, a New Testament professor, writes: "The textual evidence is against 1 John 5:7." Continuing, he writes: "Of all the Greek manuscripts, only two contain it. These two manuscripts are later, one from the fourteenth or fifteenth century and the other from the sixteenth century. Two other manuscripts have this verse written in the margin. All four manuscripts show that this verse is translated from a late form of the Latin Vulgate." [1]

"The Expositor's Bible Commentary also dismisses the King James and New King James Versions' additions in 1 John 5:7-8 as "obviously a late gloss with no merit." [2] Peake's Commentary on the Bible reads: "The famous interpolation after 'three witnesses' is not printed in RSV and rightly so] ... No respectable Greek [manuscript] contains it. Appearing first in a late 4th-century Latin text, it entered the Vulgate [the 5th-century Latin version, which became the common medieval translation] and finally, NT [New Testament] of Erasmus [who produced newly collated Greek texts and a new Latin version in the 16th century]". [3] The Big Book of Bible Difficulties reads: "This verse has virtually no support among the early Greek manuscripts..." "Its appearance in late Greek manuscripts is based on the fact that Erasmus was placed under ecclesiastical pressure to include it in his Greek NT of 1522, having omitted it in his two earlier editions of 1516 and 1519 because he could not find any Greek manuscripts which contained it." [4]

Many Trinitarian commentators agree that the addition of the words *"the Father, the Word, and the Holy Ghost: and these three are one. And there are three that bear witness in earth"* is a late addition. (See also Adam Clarke's Commentary, A Commentary by Robert Jamieson, A.R. Fausset, and David Brown) The overwhelming consensus among translators, commentators, and historians is that the words do not belong in the text.

Footnotes Chapter 15

1. How We Got the Bible, 2003, pp. 100-101

2. The Expositor's Bible Commentary, Glenn Barker, Vol. 12, 1981, p. 353

3. Peake's Commentary on the Bible, pg. 1038

4. The Big Book of Bible Difficulties, Norman Geisler and Thomas Howe, 2008, pp. 540-541

Chapter 16
Conclusion

Humankind did not always believe in a trinity. There is substantial historical evidence supporting the belief that early civilizations held to the belief in only one God. One writer stated: "In the early ages of mankind, the existence of a sole and omnipotent Deity, who created all things, seems to have been the universal belief." (1)

Hindus, Goths, Egyptians, and many other peoples of the world once believed in One God. Those same people today believe in many gods, polytheism. Interestingly, one of the most dominant and widespread forms of polytheism is a belief in not two or four gods but a trinity, three gods. Alexander Hislop wrote in The Two Babylons: "In the unity of that one only God of the Babylonians, there were three persons, and to symbolize that doctrine of the Trinity, they employed the equilateral triangle in the monastery of the so-called Trinitarians of Madrid, an image of the triune God, with three heads on one body." "In India, the supreme divinity, in like manner, in one of the most ancient cave-temples, is represented with three heads on one body, under the name of "Eko Deva Trimurtti." One god, three forms. "In Japan, the Buddhists worship their great divinity, Buddha, with three heads, in the very same form, under the name of 'San Fao Fuh'."(2)

In Egypt, we find a trinity of Osiris, Horus, and Isis. In Greece, the trinity was Zeus, Apollo, and Athena. In India, it is Brahma, Vishnu, and Shiva. The Roman "Capitoline Triad" is comprised of Jupiter (father), Juno (wife), and Minerva (daughter). Taoism has "Three Pure Ones." Even the Gnostics had a trinity of divine thought: the Father, the Son, and the Mother (Sophia). The idea of a trinity is not peculiar to Christianity. A trinity of various gods and goddesses has existed throughout recorded history. One exception was Israel.

Regarding the Trinity, the Jews believe: "The raising of Jesus to the position of divinity proceeded step by step and not without a struggle. While at first he was considered a man miraculously born of the power of the Spirit of God, elevated by God after his death and resurrection to divine dignity, the church father Tertullian (about 200) distinguished three persons combined into one substance. "The difference between person and substance already at that time was difficult to comprehend." "The designation of the third person of the Trinity, the Holy Ghost, stems from a Hebrew figure of speech, the ruah HaKodesh (holy spirit). In Jewish usage, however, this concept was never identified with a separate person...." The article continues, "Medieval Jewish philosophy always attacked the Trinity by pointing to the impossibility of equating three with one." (3) This article rightly refutes the church's attempt to use Old Testament Biblical passages to prove the Trinity. But in rejecting the Trinity (correctly), the Jews also rejected Jesus Christ as God incarnate, their Messiah (wrongly).

The word of God taught and warned them to serve the one true God, not to worship or serve idols. Israel is known throughout history for its tenacious belief in only one God. While some ancient and modern theologians have sought a Trinity in the Old Testament, none exists. The Old Testament has no such belief among the Jews or in their sacred writings. Importantly, neither Jesus nor the apostles taught the doctrine of the Trinity.

Interestingly, many Jews closest to the birth, life, and ministry of Jesus believed He was the Messiah, the incarnate

God. The following statements are from two world-renowned Jews of Jesus' day: the Apostles Thomas and Paul. Thomas said: *"And Thomas answered and said unto him, My Lord and my God."* (John 20:28). And Paul, writing in Titus 2:13, wrote: *"Looking for that blessed hope, and the glorious appearing of the great God and our Saviour Jesus Christ:"* One of the Jewish prophets proclaimed: *"For unto us a child is born, unto us a son is given: and the government shall be upon his shoulder: and his name shall be called Wonderful, Counsellor, The mighty God, The everlasting Father, The Prince of Peace."* (Isaiah 9:6). While the prophet Isaiah recognized the son as the "everlasting father," neither Isaiah nor any other Jewish writer mentions the Trinity. How is it possible that the Jews did not know about the Trinity? If God were a trinity, why didn't the Jews or Apostles (also Jews) use plural pronouns, e.g., they, them, theirs, we, or us, when referring to God? They didn't use them because they understood God is one!

Over the centuries, Jews were persecuted, murdered, cursed, shunned, slandered, and abused because they believed in one God. This separated them from the pagan nations around them. While Egypt had a different god for every aspect of nature and every locale, Israel held to one God! When Israel took over the promised land, they were told to destroy all the people, their idols, and their shrines. A Jewish Christian friend once remarked, "Israel did not change Gods at Calvary." No, the God of the Old Testament and the God of the New Testament are the same, the Lord Jesus Christ. Those that defend the doctrine of the Trinity are left with as many problems as they began with, namely this...."Who is Jesus Christ?" The problem becomes apparent when we read an explanation of the Trinity: "A doctrine so defined can be spoken of as a Biblical doctrine only on the principle that the sense of scripture is scripture.

And the definition of a Biblical doctrine in such un-Biblical language can be justified only on the principle that it is better to preserve the truth of scripture than the words of scripture." (4). The author states the "truth of scripture" is to be preserved even if we lose the "words." The author openly acknowledges the need to use "un-Biblical language" to explain the Trinity.

Protestant theologian Karl Barth (as quoted in The New International Dictionary of New Testament Theology, 1976) writes: "The New Testament does not contain the developed doctrine of the Trinity. The Bible lacks the express declaration that the Father, the Son, and the Holy Spirit are of equal essence." Trinitarians admit the Trinity is not in the Bible. The following are several quotes from scholarly publications that show this: "No Trinitarian doctrine is explicitly taught in the Old Testament. Sophisticated Trinitarians grant this, holding that the doctrine was revealed by God only later, in New Testament times (c.50–c.100) and/or in the Patristic era (c. 100–800). They usually also add, though, that with hindsight, we can see that many texts either portray or foreshadow the co-working of the Father, Son, and Holy Spirit."(5) While the doctrine of the Trinity may be "inferred" in the scriptures, Oneness (monotheism) is explicitly taught in scripture.

The entry Trinity, in the New Encyclopedia Britannica, reads: "... the doctrine of God taught by Christianity that asserts that God is one in essence but three in 'person': Father, Son, and Holy Spirit. Neither the word Trinity nor the explicit doctrine appears in the New Testament, nor did Jesus and his followers intend to contradict the Shema in the Old Testament: *"Hear, 0 Israel: The Lord our God is one Lord"* (Deuteronomy 6:4). (6)

The New Bible Dictionary reads: "The term 'Trinity' is not itself found in the Bible. It was first used by Tertullian [one of the early Catholic church theologians] at the close of the 2nd century, but received wide currency and formal elucidation only in the 4th and 5th centuries". The same source writes, "the formal doctrine of the Trinity was the result of several inadequate attempts to explain who and what the Christian God really is... To address these problems, the Church Fathers met in 325 at the Council of Nicaea to establish an orthodox biblical definition of the divine identity. However, it was not until 381, "at the Council of Constantinople, [that] the divinity of the Spirit was affirmed." (7) The Encyclopedia Americana reads: "Fourth-century Trinitarianism did not reflect accurately early Christian teaching regarding the nature of God; it was, on the contrary, a deviation from this teaching." (8) Many noted men of the church have consistently acknowledged that neither the word "trinity" nor the doctrine of the Trinity is in the Bible. And they acknowledge it is not explicitly taught in the Bible. Despite this, it remains a touchstone of orthodoxy. It has become the majority view. Tertullian wrote something very telling: "The simple, indeed, (I will not call them unwise and unlearned,) who always constitute the majority of believers, are startled at the dispensation (of the Three in One), on the ground that their very rule of faith withdraws them from the world's plurality of gods to the one only true God ..." (9) Tertullian believed the majority, though "simple," did not accept the "three in one" teaching. In Tertullian's day, it was true; most believers were Oneness.

Neither the word Trinity nor the doctrine of the Trinity is found in the Bible. The Apostles, all Jews, never mentioned it in their inspired writings. Neither did the early church leaders. Eerdmans points out: "Before the Council of Nicaea (AD 325), all theologians viewed the Son as in one way or another subordinate to the Father. Around AD 250, a dispute between Dionysius of Rome and Dionysius of Alexandria illustrated the different approaches of the churches in the West and East. The West was stronger on the unity of God and weaker on the permanent distinctness of the three; in the East, the position was reversed." (10) (See Appendix B for additional references).

The doctrine of the Trinity was an emerging, evolving, and disputed doctrine that took hundreds of years to define. Despite these facts, the church has embraced it as a "touchstone" of orthodoxy. Though the Trinity has become orthodox in the church, the reality is this: few Christians understand it. A recent survey (2016) that only included "evangelical" Christians, i.e., they believed the Bible to be their highest authority and believed in personal evangelism, revealed that seventy percent believed "Jesus was the first being God created." Twenty-eight percent did not believe the "third person of the Trinity" was "equal with God the Father of Jesus ..." (Lifeway survey as quoted by thefederalist.com). These results suggest that many evangelical believers do not understand the Trinity, as both beliefs contradict the doctrine.

A final question remains. Who do you say Jesus Christ is? The second person in the Trinity or the incarnation of the one true God? In the Scriptures, the answer is clear; Jesus Christ is not the second person in the Godhead. Jesus Christ is God manifest in the flesh.

Footnotes on Chapter 16

1. A. Hislop, The Two Babylons, page 14 Loizeaux Brothers, 1959

2. Ibid. Pgs. 16,18

3. The Universal Jewish Encyclopedia (1943), Vol. 10, pg. 308

4. The International Standard Bible Encyclopedia (1943), Vol. 5, pg. 3012

5. Stanford Encyclopedia of Philosophy, History of Trinitarian Doctrines, 2.1 The New Testament

6. New Encyclopedia Britannica, 1979, Trinity, Vol. X, p. 126

7. New Bible Dictionary, 1996, Trinity

8. The Encyclopedia Americana, p. 1956, p. 294

9. Tertullian, Against Praxeas, III

10. Eerdmans' Handbook to the History of Christianity, 1977, p. 112-113

Appendix A

Heresy

"They that approve a private opinion, call it opinion; but they that mislike it, heresy: and yet heresy signifies no more than private opinion." Thomas Hobbes 1588-1679

Undoubtedly, some believe anyone who rejects the Trinity is a heretic. Are they? The word heresy originally meant (in Greek) "being able, choice, or thing chosen." Greek usage referred to a young person and their "being able" to "choose" what philosophy they would follow in life. Over time, the word heresy changed. It became: *"any belief or theory strongly at variance with established beliefs or customs, in particular, the accepted beliefs of a church or religious organization. A heretic is a proponent of such claims or beliefs."* (Dictionary.com). By this standard of heresy, the first believers in Jesus would have been considered heretics in the eyes of the Jews because they disagreed with the law of Moses; rejected the priesthood, animal sacrifices, circumcision, etc. Were they heretics? Based on the latter definition of the word heresy, they were. However, the question should not be "were they heretics"; it should be "were they wrong?"

The early church eventually had to decide on the orthodox view of Jesus Christ. To do this, they had to establish a standard of beliefs. Lacking a standard of established beliefs lent itself to an ever-increasing number of different beliefs and practices. What was the correct doctrine? Who would decide what was correct and what was heretical? It would not be easy, as there were many conflicting views among early Christians, as there are today.

If the church considered an idea heretical at one time, it would always be heretical. That is not how heresy "works" in the church. It turns out heresy is fluid, changing, and adapting. This is borne out by many instances where the Catholic church changed its "mind" on what was or was not heretical. For example, the Catholic church taught that "outside the church, there is no salvation." Pope Boniface VIII, in his Papal Bull Unam Sanctam (A.D. 1302), wrote: "We declare, say, define, and pronounce that it is absolutely necessary for the salvation of every human creature to be subject to the Roman Pontiff."

The Popes, beginning with Boniface VIII and continuing through Pius XII (1939-1958), all confirmed this belief. Therefore, the Catholic church considered anyone who was a Protestant heretical. That changed in 1962 at the Second Vatican Council. With the stroke of a pen, Protestants were no longer heretics. Now, they were called "separated brethren." One of the most famous examples of how heresy could change involved Galileo. His heretical belief? Like Copernicus before him, he believed in a "heliocentric" universe, i.e., the Sun lies motionless at the centre of the universe, that the Earth is not at its centre and moves...." The church insisted that he "abjure, curse and detest" his ideas, while it insisted the Earth was the center of the Universe (https://en.wikipedia.org/wiki/Galileo_Galilei)

The "heliocentric" belief, initially the idea of Copernicus, had been labeled heresy in 1616. Later, Galileo, using a telescope, came to believe Copernicus was right. He was deemed a heretic in 1633 and placed under house arrest until his death. In judging Galileo, the council determined he was "vehemently suspected of heresy." The church believed the idea of the Earth moving around the Sun was "foolish and absurd in philosophy, and formally heretical since it explicitly contradicts in many places the sense of Scripture"(https://en.wikipedia.org/wiki/Galileo_Galilei). In the Spring of 1633, Galileo recanted.

Three hundred and seventy-six years later, in 1992, the church admitted it was wrong. But the admission did not come easily. The church only concluded Galileo was right after a 13-year investigation! So, Galileo was no longer a heretic? Galileo was a heretic. Not because he was wrong, he was right, but because he disagreed with the established religious belief of his day. Remember, a heretic is someone who disagrees with an established belief. As determined by the church, heresy is not a question of what is right or wrong according to the scriptures. Heresy in the church was always determined by the one who held power, whether Emperors or Popes. The point is this: "established beliefs" may be wrong. If the established beliefs are false, then labeling someone who does not accept them as a heretic becomes meaningless.

Appendix B

Additional Notes on the Trinity

"Neither the word Trinity nor the explicit doctrine appears in the New Testament, nor did Jesus and his followers intend to contradict the Shema in the Hebrew Scriptures: *'Hear, O Israel: The Lord our God is one Lord"* (Deuteronomy 6:4). (Britannica.com/topic/Trinity-Christianity)

"The doctrine of the Holy Trinity is not taught [explicitly] in the [Old Testament], ... The formulation "one God in three Persons' was not solidly established [by a council] ... prior to the end of the 4th century." (New Catholic Encyclopedia (1967) Vol. XIV, p. 299).

"The doctrine of the Trinity is purely a revealed doctrine. That is to say, it embodies a truth which has never been discovered and is indiscoverable by natural reason. With all his searching, man has not been able to find out for himself the deepest things of God. Accordingly, ethnic thought has never attained a Trinitarian conception of God, nor does any ethnic religion present in its representations of the divine being any analogy to the doctrine of the Trinity" (The International Standard Bible Encyclopedia, Vol. 5, Trinity 2, pg. 3012, 1939).

"The New Testament contains no explicit Trinitarian doctrine. However, many Christian theologians, apologists, and philosophers hold that the doctrine can be inferred from what the New Testament does teach about God" (Stanford Encyclopedia of Philosophy, History of Trinitarian Doctrines, 2.2 The New Testament).

"Theologians today are in agreement that the Hebrew Bible does not contain a doctrine of the Trinity" (The Encyclopedia of Religion Vol. 15 1987, pages 53-57).

"The fact of the matter is that the Bible does not teach the Trinity. The opening words of The Oxford Companion to the Bible under the article "Trinity" are enlightening: "Because the Trinity is such an important part of later Christian doctrine, it is striking that the term does not appear in the New Testament. Likewise, the developed concept of three coequal partners in the Godhead found in later creedal formulations cannot be detected within the confines of the [New Testament] canon" (Bruce Metzger and Michael Coogan, editors, 1993, p. 782).

Appendix C

The Beliefs

In the post-apostolic years, there were many ideas concerning who Jesus was. These beliefs began to increase throughout the empire. Here are some of the dominant ones:

Subordinationists:

The belief is that the Son and the Holy Spirit are subordinate to the Father.

Monarchians:

Monarchians are commonly associated with Sabellianism, the view that One God appears in three modes. Some historians believe this was the dominant belief among Christians in the 3rd century. They point out that Tertullian mentioned this in his writing "Against Praxeas, Chapter 3".

Montanism:

It was a Christian sect founded in the second century by Montanus. There were two noted prophetesses, Maximilla and Priscilla (Prisca). Their fundamental belief: the Holy Spirit would speak through them using ecstatic utterances and prophecies. Unlike the prophets of old, who would preface their prophecies with "thus sayeth the Lord," they spoke as though they were God: "I am the Father, the Word, and the Paraclete" (Didymus, "De Trin." III, xli). Perhaps the most notable adherent was Tertullian.

Patripassianism: (Latin patri-"father passio-"suffering"):

In this belief, the Father, having become incarnate in Christ, suffered at the crucifixion. This belief may have contributed to the idea of "separate" or "distinct" persons in the Godhead, as they knew God could not be crucified. Some believe this is a "form" of Sabellianism.

Sabellianism (see also Modalism and Patripassianism):

The term Sabellianism comes from Sabellius, a theologian and priest from the 3rd century. The problem we face is this: none of his writings have survived. What we know of him and his beliefs comes from opponents. According to them, he believed in one God who revealed Himself in three different "modes." He opposed the Trinitarian belief in three distinct persons. What distinguishes Oneness believers today from Sabellianism is this: Sabellians believed that God appeared in only one "mode" at a time. Oneness believes God can appear in numerous modes or manifestations simultaneously.

Appendix D

Jehovah's Witnesses:

The Jehovah's Witnesses made too many additions and changes to the scriptures in their New World Translation to put in the book. Instead, I placed some of the more egregious ones in an Appendix. To support their rejection of hell and their belief in annihilation, they translated the Greek word "kolasis" as "cutting off" instead of "punishment" (Matthew 25:46).

In John 8:58, the Greek words "ego eimi," meaning "I am," are translated as "I have been." They did this to conceal Jesus' claim of being the "I Am" God of Israel. (Exodus 3:14, John 8:58).

In John 14:14, the word "me" is omitted in "ask Me anything."

In Acts 2:28, they put the word "son" in "blood of his own [son]" in brackets without any support in the Greek text. This was done to obscure the deity of Jesus Christ.

In Hebrews 1:8, the phrase "Your throne, O God" is replaced with "God is your throne" to obscure the fact that the Hebrews writer identifies Jesus as God by quoting Psalms 45:6 and applying it directly to the Son of God.

In Isaiah 30:29, the Greek phrase, "he petra de en ho Kristos," meaning "and the rock was Christ," is mistranslated as "and that rock-mass meant the Christ." Again, this shifts the focus from Jesus being God, the Rock of Israel (1 Corinthians 10:4).

In the 1984 edition of the New World Translation, the word "other" has been inserted into the text in brackets, e.g., [other]. They did this to suggest the word does not appear in the original Greek text. The use of brackets is correct, as the word does not appear in the Greek text. An example occurs in their translation of Philippians 2:9. First, we read the KJV "Wherefore God also hath highly exalted him and given him a name which is above every name:" Here is the Watchtower's version: "gave him the name that is above every [other] name." The addition of the word "other" was done to support their teaching that the name "Jehovah" is superior to the name "Jesus." However, all editions of their translation before 1981 and after 2006 have the word "other" in the text without the brackets. Removing the brackets leads the reader to believe the word "other" is in the original Greek text. It is not.

Here is another example of their "sleight of hand" exegesis of the scriptures in Colossians 1:15-17: "He is the image of the invisible God, the firstborn of all creation because by means of him all **other** things were created in the heavens and upon the earth.... All **other** things have been created through him and for him. Also, he is before all **other** things, and by means of him all **other** things were made to exist." Here is the same quote in the KJV: *"Who is the image of the invisible God, the firstborn of every creature: For by him were all things created, that are in heaven, and that are in earth, visible and invisible, whether they be thrones, or dominions, or principalities, or powers: all things were created by him, and for him: And he is before all things, and by him all things consist."* They inserted the word "other" four times with no support as it is not in the original Greek text. Why did they do this? By inserting the word "other," they make it appear that Jesus is the same as "other" created beings.

In Colossians 2:9, the Greek word "Theotetos," meaning "Godship, Deity, Godhead," is mistranslated as "divine quality" to detract from the full Deity of God being attributed to Christ in this passage.

In Titus 2:13, the Greek phrase "Theou kai Soteros emon," meaning "God and Savior of us" or "our God and Savior," is mistranslated as "god and of [the] Savior of us." The word "the," being inserted in brackets with no basis in the Greek text, is yet another attempt by NWT translators to mislead the reader.

In Hebrews 12:9,23, the Greek words "pneumaton" and "pneumas," meaning "spirits," are mistranslated as "spiritual life" and "spiritual lives" to support the

Watchtower belief that denies the existence of the human "spirit" that lives on after death.

In Acts 20:28, NWT reads: "Pay attention to yourselves and to all the flock, among which the holy spirit has appointed you overseers, to shepherd the congregation of God, which he purchased with **the blood of his own Son.**" Let's compare their translation with the original quote. We can readily see their bias: "Take heed therefore unto yourselves, and to all the flock, over the which the Holy Ghost hath made you overseers, **to feed the church of God, which he hath purchased with his own blood.**" The Witnesses changed the phrase "with His own blood" to "the blood of his own Son."

Young's Literal Translation has, "Take heed, therefore, to yourselves, and to all the flock, among which the Holy Spirit made you overseers, **to feed the assembly of God that He acquired through His blood,**" The American Standard Version has "... Take heed unto yourselves, and to all the flock, in which the Holy Spirit hath made you bishops, **to feed the church of the Lord which he purchased with his own blood.**" Virtually all other versions, except the New World Translation, translate this passage correctly. The original text tells the reader that God purchased the church with His blood!

In John 1:18, we see their sleight of hand again: "No man has seen God at any time; the only-**begotten god**, who is at the Father's side, is the one who has explained Him." (NWT) Notice the word "god" is lowercase in their translation. The word "god" does not even appear in the original text. They added it. Here is the passage from the Greek text: *"No man hath seen God at any time; the only begotten Son, which is in the bosom of the Father, he hath* *declared him."* They translate the word "son" in the original text as "god" (lowercase) with no textual support. In the Greek text, the word is "huios" and should be translated as "son." The word for "God" in this passage is "theos," not "huios" (son). In doing this, they mean to suggest, again, that the "begotten son" is "a god."

One of their translation rules concerns passages where the New Testament quotes the Old Testament. Here is their rule: "In places where the Christian Greek Scripture writers quote the earlier Hebrew Scriptures, the translator has the right to render the word κυριος (kurios) as 'Jehovah' wherever the divine name appeared in the Hebrew original." [This rule is found in an official Watchtower publication, The Divine Name That Will Endure Forever (1984), pages 26-27]. In other words, if the New Testament is quoting from the Old Testament and the Old Testament passage uses the Hebrew word Jehovah. The New Testament quotation should also use the word Jehovah.

An example of this is in Romans 10:13, which is a quotation from Joel 2:32 where the word Jehovah is found: *"And it shall come to pass that whosoever shall call on the name of the LORD (Jehovah) shall be delivered"* (Joel 2:32, KJV). Here is the New World Translation of this passage: "And it must occur that everyone who calls on the name of Jehovah will get away safe" (New World Translation of Joel 2:32). Since the Old Testament passage contained Jehovah, so should the New Testament companion scripture; "Everyone who calls on the name of Jehovah will be saved" (New World Translation of Romans 10:13). Here they faithfully followed their own rule and translated the Greek word "Kyrios" (Lord) as Jehovah. However, there are at least two examples where they violated their own rule:

Philippians 2:10-11 *"That at the name of Jesus every knee should bow, of things in heaven, and things in earth, and things under the earth; and that every tongue should confess that **Jesus Christ is Lord,** to the glory of God the Father."* (Phil. 2:10-11, emphasis mine) This quote is based on Isaiah 45:23. Though Paul does not quote the Old Testament passage word for word, there is no question that Paul had this passage in mind. Isaiah 45:23 reads, *"I have sworn by myself, the word is gone out of my mouth in righteousness, and shall not return, That unto me every knee shall bow, every tongue shall swear."* Isaiah said that every knee would bow to God. Paul, referring to this same passage in Isaiah, wrote that every knee would bow to Jesus Christ. Paul wrote in verse 11 that every tongue would someday confess that Jesus is Lord (kurios); that is, everyone will eventually acknowledge that Jesus is, according to the Jehovah's Witnesses' rule, "Jehovah" the true God! But Jehovah's Witnesses refuse to translate "Lord" in the Philippian passage as Jehovah. However, it is evident that Jehovah is the One referred to in the context of Isaiah 45:23. The New World Translation renders it this way: "and every tongue should openly acknowledge that Jesus Christ is Lord to the glory of God the Father." Their Bible translation is eager to render "Lord" as "Jehovah" whenever it suits their objective (237 times in the N.T.). Still, here they cannot do so because it would force them to acknowledge that Jesus is God.

Paul also quotes from Isaiah 45:23. It is found in Romans 14:11, "For it is written, As I live, saith the Lord, every knee shall bow to me, and every tongue shall confess **to God**" emphasis mine). Here is how the Jehovah's Witnesses translate this passage: "for it is written: 'As I live,' says Jehovah, '**to me** every knee will bend down, and every tongue will make open acknowledgment to God." (New World Translation of Rom. 14:11, emphasis mine). By using

Jehovah in their translation of Rom. 14:11, the Jehovah's Witnesses acknowledge that the Isaiah 45:23 passage indeed refers to God. But when Paul uses the same quote in Philippians 2:11, they did not translate "Lord" as "Jehovah." In this case, following their own rule would result in a translation that would destroy the very foundation of their cult. Their faith is based on the faulty foundation of a defective view of Christ that Christ is a mere creature (an exalted angel) and not the Creator-God. They deny the deity of our Lord and Saviour.

The second verse is 1 Peter 2:3 *"If so be ye have tasted that the Lord is gracious"* (1 Peter 2:3). Bible scholars agree that Peter was quoting from Psalms 34:8 *"Oh taste and see that the LORD (Jehovah) is good"* (KJV). Those familiar with Greek can compare the Septuagint translation of Psalms 34:8 with the Greek of 1 Peter 2:3 and find that the language is almost identical. For example, the Greek words for "good" and "gracious" are the same: "chrēstos." The Psalmist gave the invitation: *"Oh taste and see that the LORD is good (gracious)."*

Remember the translation rule that the Jehovah's Witnesses use; if the divine name appears in the Hebrew original (and it does appear in Psalms 34:8), then the translator must render the word "kurios" as Jehovah. However, in their translation of 1 Peter 2:3, they, again, violate their own rule: "provided you have tasted that the **Lord** is kind" (1 Pet. 2:3 New World Translation.

www.ingramcontent.com/pod-product-compliance
Lightning Source LLC
Chambersburg PA
CBHW061643040426
42446CB00010B/1548